05 JUL 2013

- 4 DEC 2019

**THE LONDON BOROUGH**
www.bromley.gov.uk

## Biggin Hill
## 01959 574468

Please return/renew this item
by the last date shown
Books may be renewed by
phone

D1353911

30128 80075 188 8

Published in the UK and USA
in 2012 by Icon Books Ltd,
Omnibus Business Centre,
39–41 North Road,
London N7 9DP
email: info@iconbooks.co.uk
www.iconbooks.co.uk

Sold in the UK, Europe,
South Africa and Asia
by Faber & Faber Ltd,
Bloomsbury House,
74–77 Great Russell Street,
London WC1B 3DA or their agents

Distributed in the UK, Europe,
South Africa and Asia by TBS Ltd,
TBS Distribution Centre,
Colchester Road, Frating Green,
Colchester CO7 7DW

Published in Australia in 2012
by Allen & Unwin Pty Ltd,
PO Box 8500,
83 Alexander Street,
Crows Nest,
NSW 2065

Distributed in Canada
by Penguin Books Canada,
90 Eglinton Avenue East, Suite 700,
Toronto,
Ontario M4P 2Y3

Distributed to the trade in the USA
by Consortium Book Sales
and Distribution,
The Keg House,
34 Thirteenth Avenue NE,
Suite 101,
Minneapolis, MN 55413-1007

ISBN: 978-184831-401-6

Typeset in Avenir by Marie Doherty

Printed and bound in the UK by Clays Ltd, St Ives plc

# About the authors

**Alison Price** is a Chartered Occupational Psychologist who has worked with thousands of employees to help them realize their potential at work. Alison specializes in Leadership and Management Development, working with managers of all levels, including senior managers of prestigious organizations.

In 2009, Alison was a semi-finalist in 'Britain's Next Top Coach'. Alison also lectures on a master's-level course in Business Psychology at a London university. She offers her services through her company The Success Agents.

**David Price** is a senior manager and has led award-winning teams within prestigious financial services organizations. David has qualifications in management and coaching, and is a qualified Member of the Chartered Management Institute.

Further information about the authors and resources on management can be found at the following website:

www.management-handbook.com

# Authors' note

This book contains frequently used research and methods. Where we know the source we have been sure to reference it, but our apologies here to the originators of any material if we have overlooked them.

# Dedication

This book is dedicated to all of our family, friends and acquaintances who contributed their stories and completed the management assessment.

Also, we would like to say thank you to all bad managers everywhere, who provided the suffering that produced many of the stories and inspired much of this book.

We hope that this book will result in us never hearing a bad management story again.

# Contents

About the authors                                            iii
Authors' note                                                 iv
Dedication                                                    iv

Introduction                                                   1

A: Assessment                                                  6
B: Basics                                                     17
C: Communication                                             24
D: Distributing work                                         32
E: Empowerment                                               41
F: Feedback                                                  49
G: Goal-setting                                              57
H: Hiring                                                    64
 I: Induction                                                74
J: Justice                                                   81
K: Kindness                                                  89
 L: Life–work balance                                        96
M: Managing change                                          104
N: Not coping                                               112
O: Operational problems                                     119
P: Poor performance                                         127
Q: Quarrels                                                 138
R: Respect                                                  146
S: Strengths                                                153

T: Training                               161
U: Upward progression                     170
V: Values                                 177
W: Well done                              186
X: eXtra effort                           194
Y: Your personality                       204
Z: Zone of successful management          211

Acknowledgements                          218

# Introduction

A decade of experience in designing, delivering and evaluating management training has made us realize that what is taught in a classroom, or covered in a typical management textbook, can sound great in theory but doesn't always translate to the real world.

For example, many managers will have been taught about the importance of setting SMART objectives (ones that are Specific, Measurable, Achievable, Realistic and Time-bound) to focus employees on the things that matter. However, how much use are perfectly worded objectives if employees don't actually look at them until the night before their annual appraisal, at which point they have to conjure up as much evidence as possible to show that they *really* have been focused on them *all* year?

This book is therefore grounded in reality, covering not only how to perform management activities appropriately but, crucially, how to make them work in the real world. It shares very practical (and easily applied) solutions to issues that managers and their employees face on a day-to-day basis.

To achieve this, we've interviewed many people, seeking to answer the following questions:

1. **How can managers make a really positive difference to members of their team?** This book is packed with

examples of good practice that you can easily replicate within your own team to ensure that everyone thrives.

2. **What have managers done in real life that absolutely crushed their team or individuals within it?** During the research for this book we have been genuinely shocked at how easy it was to gather a wealth of horror stories, showing just how common management bad-practice is. For example, one interviewee described how her colleague received an absolutely devastating phone call to say that, very sadly, her aunt had committed suicide. Shockingly, their manager's response was: 'Could you just focus on your work for 24 more hours and worry about your family issues later?' This book contains numerous real-life examples, and will give you very blunt (and hopefully helpful) feedback on what *not* to do as a manager.

3. **What do managers find really hard about their role and what would they like to be able to do better?** Being a manager isn't easy. It can be very tough to tell a member of your team that they aren't performing up to the required standard, or to manage the expectations of someone who is desperate to be promoted when there's simply no opportunity to do so at the time. This guide will support you to overcome these challenges and many others, exposing the difficult aspects of management and, crucially, how to deal with them competently.

In addition to interviewing managers and employees, we've also surveyed them. This forms the basis of Chapter A: 'Assessment', and gives you the opportunity to measure and calibrate your own management capability. Since each question in the survey relates to an individual chapter in the book, you can use your survey results to prioritize which chapters to read first in order to identify areas for growth. You can then repeat the survey, say in three months' time, and use it as a way to measure your progress.

## Who will benefit from this book?

This Practical Guide to management is designed to benefit three key groups of people the most:

1. **Newly appointed managers.** People are frequently promoted to a managerial position because they are technically good at their job, yet being a manager requires an entirely different skill-set. If you want a succinct and easy-to-apply guide to developing that skill-set, read on!

2. **Experienced managers.** In 2009 a British national newspaper ran a story saying that 50% of experienced UK drivers would fail their driving test if they took it again. This isn't because we Brits are useless drivers! Instead it reflects the fact that we learn to drive subconsciously and therefore pay less attention to doing everything right – and so we develop bad habits. The same is true

for management. When you're a newly appointed manager, you may be very conscious about how you interact with and manage your team. However, over time, you can pick up bad habits, and things that you might once have made a real effort to do right are now done on autopilot. Consider this book as a *metaphorical driving test*, making you consciously aware of what you're doing, and challenging you to double-check that you aren't displaying any major or minor faults.

3. **Aspiring managers.** If you have aspirations to become a manager, this book is a great starting point. You'll find that the vast majority of exercises are designed so that both managers and non-managers can complete them – and we wish you the best of luck with getting that promotion!

It's not only the manager who will feel the benefit of good management – organizations will too. A research report from the Chartered Management Institute (2012) highlights the benefits that improved manager capability brings, and why management development is so important.

The report found that high-performing organizations reported higher levels of management effectiveness compared to low-performing organizations. There is evidence that there's a virtuous cycle between the ability of its managers and the performance of the organization. With 43% of managers in the research rated as ineffective and 63%

of managers not having any formal training for their role, organizations – and all those who have a stake in their future – stand to be able to benefit from developing better, more effective managers.

## The A–Z to management

You may have noticed that each of our chapters links to a different letter of the alphabet. In our home country, the United Kingdom, an A–Z is a map book – something that helps people to have smooth journeys and to get back on track when things go wrong. We very much hope that our A–Z is a useful guide to you as you continue on your own management journey.

**Alison & David Price**

# A: Assessment

*It is not the strongest of the species that survives, nor the
most intelligent, but the ones most responsive to change.*
Charles Darwin

The focus of this chapter is to conduct a self-assessment of
your management capabilities, but before we do this, we
just want to provoke you into thinking that, as a manager,
you are actually being assessed all of the time, for example:

- After a bad interaction with our own manager, we often
  go home and vent to our family about how we feel. Not
  only can your manager ruin your day, he or she has the
  potential to ruin your family's too!
- We frequently judge how fairly we are being treated in
  comparison to our peers, and we can feel very disgruntled when we sense injustice.
- And we're guessing that virtually everyone will admit to
  going to lunch or socializing after work with peers and
  having a detailed conversation about our manager!

So, imagine that you're a fly on the wall listening to that
conversation about you. Would you like what you hear, or
would the truth hurt?

Managers can literally make or break an employee's
job satisfaction. Their impact extends far beyond the office
doors. For example, only yesterday an employee told us

that she's currently having professional counselling due to a difficult relationship with her manager.

When you become a manager, not only do you take on the responsibility for getting the work of the team done, but you become someone who has a significant emotional impact on other people's lives. It's often said that 'People don't leave organizations, they leave managers'.

We want your employees to say great things about you in the pub after work. So to start you (or maintain you) on that track, we've provided a self-assessment to help you evaluate your management capability. You will also have an opportunity to rate your own manager.

---

 For each of the following questions, rate your own manager between 1 and 5. 1 = strongly disagree; 5 = strongly agree.

| A | My manager is a good manager. | |
|---|---|---|
| B | I know what is expected of me at work and I have the working conditions/equipment that I need to do my job. | |
| C | The way my manager communicates with me has a positive impact upon my attitude and performance. | |
| D | The distribution of workload between members of the team is fair. | |
| E | When team members are willing and capable, our manager gives them the freedom to be in control of their own work. | |

| F | I am given useful and accurate feedback about my performance on a regular basis. | |
|---|---|---|
| G | My manager helps me to set goals and objectives at work that motivate me. | |
| H | When vacancies in this team are filled, the process is fair and leads to the appointment of suitable people. | |
| I | New starters to the team are given the support, resources and information they need. | |
| J | Members of the team are treated fairly in comparison to each other by our manager. | |
| K | My manager is supportive when I have personal issues outside of work. | |
| L | I have an acceptable work–life balance. | |
| M | My manager is good at supporting me during times of change. | |
| N | I am under an acceptable level of pressure at work. | |
| O | My manager is effective at work-related problem-solving. | |
| P | Poor performance is dealt with effectively by my manager. | |
| Q | My manager has a positive impact in conflict situations. | |
| R | My manager treats and speaks to me respectfully at work. | |
| S | My manager enables me to play to my strengths at work. | |
| T | I have opportunities that enable me to learn and develop at work. | |

| U | I receive effective careers advice to support my personal development and progression. | |
|---|---|---|
| V | My manager understands and is supportive of the things that are important to me. | |
| W | I am adequately recognized and rewarded for my contribution at work. | |
| X | I am treated in a way at work that makes me feel committed and that I want to work hard. | |
| Y | My manager's personality has a positive impact upon me. | |
| Z | My manager ensures that the team's work is done, the team as a whole is happy and individual needs are met. | |

If you currently manage a team of people, repeat the assessment, this time rating your own managerial capability. If you don't manage a team of people, you can have a guess as to how good you think you would be:

| A | I am a good manager. | |
|---|---|---|
| B | My team members know what is expected of them and have the working conditions/equipment they need to do their job. | |
| C | The way that I communicate with my team has a positive impact upon their attitude and performance. | |
| D | I distribute the workload of the team fairly between its members. | |

| E | Where team members are willing and capable, I give them the freedom to be in control of their own work. | |
|---|---|---|
| F | I give useful and accurate feedback about my team members' performance to them on a regular basis. | |
| G | I help my team members to set goals and objectives at work that motivate them. | |
| H | When vacancies in this team are filled by me, the process is fair and leads to the appointment of suitable people. | |
| I | New starters to the team are given the support, resources and information they need from me. | |
| J | Members of the team are treated fairly in comparison to each other by me. | |
| K | I am supportive of my team when they have personal issues outside of work. | |
| L | I make sure that the team has an acceptable work–life balance. | |
| M | I am good at supporting my team members during times of change. | |
| N | My team are under an acceptable level of pressure at work. | |
| O | I am effective at resolving work-related issues. | |
| P | I deal with poor performance effectively within my team. | |
| Q | I have a positive impact in conflict situations. | |
| R | I treat and speak to my team respectfully at work. | |
| S | I enable my team to play to their strengths in their work. | |

| T | I create opportunities that enable my team members to learn and develop at work. | |
|---|---|---|
| U | I provide effective careers advice to support my team's personal development and progression. | |
| V | I understand what is important to individuals in my team and support them to achieve this. | |
| W | I adequately recognize and reward my team for their contribution at work. | |
| X | I treat my team members in a way at work that makes them feel committed and that they want to work hard. | |
| Y | My personality has a positive impact upon the team. | |
| Z | I ensure that the team's work is done, the team as a whole is happy and individual needs are met. | |

---

## And the survey said ...

We asked a sample of employees and managers – from lawyers in America to government employees in the UK and personal assistants in Australia – to complete this survey. The results have been very revealing.

The two pie charts that follow show how many 1's, 2's, 3's, 4's and 5's were made across all questions, divided into the categories of employees rating their managers and managers rating themselves. The results showed that:

- **9%** of employee ratings of their managers were 1's (the worst rating) whereas **0%** of managers' ratings of themselves were 1's.

- **16%** of employee ratings were 2's whereas only **6%** of managers' ratings were 2's.
- **53%** of employee ratings were 4's and 5's whereas **73%** of managers' ratings were 4's and 5's.

So it's clear that managers rate themselves higher than employees rate their managers. Although the size of the gap between employees' and managers' ratings varied by individual question, on average, managers rated themselves 0.5 higher per question than employees rated their managers. Therefore, as a rough rule of thumb, managers should subtract 0.5 from each rating they have made about themselves. As a manager, this is likely to give you a flavour of what your team would have scored you. The breakdown of the gap by individual questions is shown on page 15.

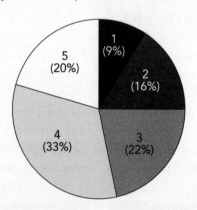

*Breakdown of all ratings from 1 (very bad) to 5 (very good) made by employees about their manager's capability.*

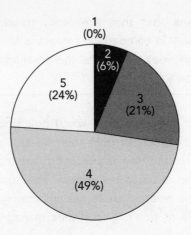

*Breakdown of all ratings from 1 (very bad) to 5 (very good) made by managers about their own capability.*

## Breakdown of data by question

The following graph shows a more detailed breakdown of the survey findings, comparing the results from both employees and managers.

The data shown is listed from the strongest to the weakest area as rated by employees. From this you will see that employees think managers are strongest at ensuring that basics are in place and weakest at managing poor performance.

Pay particular attention to how much longer the managers' bar is compared to the employees' bar. For example, the graph shows that managers think that they are really good at 'treating employees fairly in comparison to each other' (J: Justice); however, employees don't rate their managers anywhere near as positively.

---

In addition to gathering data about how good managers are at various aspects of their role, we also asked survey respondents to rate how *important* it was that their manager was good at these behaviours. The rationale behind this was to see whether there are any management areas where employees don't mind if their manager is good or not.

You will notice that over 80% of the question headings have a * or ** next to them, which shows the degree of the importance ratings. ** denotes an average score of over 4.5 out of 5.0, and * denotes anything with an average score of over 4.0.

---

Look at the graph and find:
- The three strongest areas as rated by each group.
- The three weakest areas as rated by each group.

---

■ Average score manager  ■ Average score employees

|  | |
|---|---|
| AVERAGE OF ALL DATA | |
| B – Basics * | |
| R – Respect * | |
| Z – Zone * | |
| K – Kindness * | |
| Q – Quarrels | |
| E – Empowerment ** | |
| W – Well done ** | |
| S – Strengths * | |
| O – Operational problems | |
| C – Communication * | |
| I – Induction * | |
| M – Managing change | |
| J – Justice * | |
| T – Training * | |
| X – eXtra effort * | |
| D – Distributing work * | |
| A – Assessment ** | |
| F – Feedback * | |
| N – Not coping * | |
| Y – Your personality | |
| L – Life–work balance * | |
| H – Hiring * | |
| V – Values | |
| U – Upward progression * | |
| G – Goals * | |
| P – Poor performance * | |

1.0    2.0    3.0    4.0    5.0

## Next steps

If you currently manage a team of people, you can ask individuals within your team to complete the survey. Then you can average their results.

As a rough rule of thumb, you should aim to achieve a minimum average of 3 in each area, and we recommend that you aim to eliminate individual ratings of 1's and 2's wherever possible. Remember that each survey question (labelled A to Z) relates directly to a chapter (also labelled A to Z) so this book will give you very focused support to improve your survey scores. As you read the book, you will find lots of examples of behaviours that would lead to ratings of 1's and 2's (to be avoided) and examples of behaviours that will help you to score 4's and 5's.

---

**IF YOU REMEMBER ONE THING** The aim of this book is to help you to feel like and be perceived as a good manager – collecting regular survey data from your team is a great way to celebrate your strengths, highlight weaker areas that you can act upon, and keep in touch with your team's feelings.

---

# B: Basics

*Most of us forget the basics and wonder why
the specifics don't work.*

Garrison Wynn

When building a house, you have to get the foundations
right. It doesn't matter how great the kitchen is if the walls
can't stand. This chapter will outline the 'foundations' for
being a great manager.

---

**THINK ABOUT IT**

To begin with, imagine that your country is
hosting a major international sporting event
and you've been offered a position as a vol-
unteer to support it. You eagerly await day
one, as you'll be involved in something really special that
the whole world is watching, working alongside thousands
of other equally excited volunteers.

However, imagine how quickly everyone's enthusiasm
could plummet if you didn't know:

- What work tasks you are meant to be doing?
- When you are meant to be working?
- When you can leave your post to take a break?
- How to use or access equipment needed to do your job?
- Who else is in your team?
- Who to report problems to?

And ask yourself, how long would you keep volunteering if you were:

- Bored from doing constantly monotonous tasks?
- Ravenous or thirsty – unable to access refreshments?
- Cold or wet, without proper protection from the elements?
- In personal danger due to unsafe working conditions?
- Bullied by other members of the workforce?

No matter how exciting the opportunity, you would be likely to get extremely fed up very quickly, and would probably consider walking out.

---

This example shows the importance of getting the basics right. Frederick Hertzberg called these basics **hygiene factors**. But why are they called that?

Think about your toilets at work. (OK, so maybe they're not what you'd like to spend your spare time thinking about, but stick with us!) When your work toilets are clean, do you walk in and leap in the air because, hooray, they're really motivating you? We think that's highly unlikely. However, if you walked into the same toilets and found them to be absolutely rancid, how would you feel then? You'd likely become very annoyed at the poor conditions in which you have to work.

In the same way that hygiene probably doesn't excite you, hygiene factors don't motivate people either. They don't make you think, 'Wow, what an amazing day, the plug I touched at work was safe!' When hygiene factors are missing, though, just like hygiene itself, it can make people feel very negative to the point where they will consider leaving their job. For example, if you were standing for hours outside in the freezing cold, making yourself ill because your uniform wasn't warm enough, you would become extremely unhappy very quickly.

Here is a list of some of the most important hygiene factors:

- Food and drink
- Rest
- Shelter
- Access to toilet facilities
- Having a manager
- Clarity over when you will work and what you will do
- Personal safety and security (including freedom from bullying and harassment)
- Access to (and ability to use) equipment necessary to perform the job
- Access to physical locations required to perform the job.

---

Let's explore the impact of a lack of some of these hygiene factors in more detail through a real-life example. Harry had been offered a part-time teaching role in a college, starting from the next academic year, which would involve him running a few scheduled classes every month. Here's what happened:

- The new academic year had started and Harry still had no idea what dates he was due to be teaching.

- When Harry tried to find this out, he was told that the person who hired him, Pam, had left the college. Pam's replacement was on maternity leave, and the person doing the maternity cover had no idea who Harry was.

- When Harry was eventually notified about his teaching dates he still had no idea where the lessons would be held, or how to use the equipment in the classroom.

- To get his staff pass Harry needed authorization from his line manager, but he didn't know who that now was.

- To get a car-parking permit Harry needed his staff pass, so when he came to run the lessons, he had to travel by bus, with the journey taking over three times as long.

- After finally arriving for his first class, Harry was thirsty. The only nearby place that he could get some water was from a cafeteria, which he couldn't access without the staff pass that he still didn't have.

How do you think Harry was feeling before he'd even started delivering his first lesson? Which of the hygiene factors listed above were missing for Harry, and why was the absence of each of these hygiene factors demotivating to him?

## How can managers get the basics right?

Some aspects of making sure the basics are right will be outside of a manager's control. For example, it's unlikely that a junior supervisor will be able to authorize the installation of a new water dispenser. However, despite some limitations, a manager can influence the basics being met. For example, managers can encourage their team members to take regular breaks, so that they have time to eat.

---

Look at the list of hygiene factors above and come up with at least one way that a manager can directly support each hygiene factor being met.

---

We will give you much more detailed information to answer this question throughout the book, but in particular, look out for the content in Chapter I: 'Induction'. This chapter will cover what needs to be put in place on day one of an employee's role, which includes ensuring that a lot of these basic needs are met.

## The psychological contract

When we sign up to work with an organization, sometimes it's made very clear that the nature of the work will mean that some of the hygiene factors won't be well met, for example the job might require access to temporary toilets, or lots of time outside in the cold and rain. Whereas these conditions might be completely unacceptable to some, others can accept this, because it's what they signed up for and they understand that this is what the job demands.

Most employees will have a written contract, which specifies their hours and their place of work, etc. However, managers should understand that there is a second form of contract, an unwritten one called the **psychological contract**, which represents a manager's and employee's mutual beliefs and agreements of what they will give to each other and expect in return. The psychological contract will begin to form during the recruitment stage as the two parties discuss what they can offer each other, and will evolve throughout the course of the working relationship.

It is important that managers do three things with regard to the psychological contract:

1.  If the nature of the job impacts on some of the hygiene factors, it is important that managers make prospective employees aware of this prior to them accepting the role. In other words, they should give them a realistic view of the role. Linking back to the volunteering example at the beginning of this chapter, if you are made aware that your job is likely to involve putting out traffic cones day after day and you are still happy to take the job, then scoring poorly against one of the hygiene factors (relief from monotonous tasks) is less of a problem.

2.  When managers know that a role will entail some down-sides, they should work extra hard to make the best out of a bad situation for their team members. For example, if you know that people are likely to find their work very boring, think about ways that you can rotate job tasks to give some variety and relief from monotony.

3.  You breach the psychological contract when you fail to deliver on what you have promised employees, and this can have a *really* negative impact on them. If you have promised someone that the basics will be in place, for example that they will have a desk when they start their new job, make sure that you follow through on this.

---

**IF YOU REMEMBER ONE THING** If a member of staff doesn't have the basic conditions to do their job, or know what's expected of them, they will quickly become dissatisfied in their role. Therefore, satisfying 'hygiene factors' is one of the most important roles of a manager.

---

# C: Communication

*They may forget what you said, but they will never forget how you made them feel.*

Carl Buechner

Have you ever played 'spot the difference', where you have to look at two almost identical pictures and try to work out the difference between them? Well, let's play spot the difference with these two different scenarios.

---

**Dave's day at the office – TAKE 1**

- Dave found out that a relative had died unexpectedly last night, so he isn't feeling his normal self. As he comes in to work his manager, Sarah, looks like she's in a bad mood and doesn't bother to say hello to him.

- Dave turns on his computer and is confronted by lots of seemingly irrelevant emails, mainly between Sarah and another team member, which Dave has been copied in to, but didn't need to be. He does find a relevant email from Sarah asking him to do a piece of work, but it's really vaguely written and he isn't sure what he needs to do. When he asks for a bit of clarification, Sarah 'bites his head off' for interrupting her, which really doesn't help, considering he isn't feeling great anyway.

24

- Dave also feels frustrated because he asked Sarah for some information by the end of the day yesterday, to help him meet an upcoming work deadline, and she hasn't responded.

- At 11.30am Dave attends the hour-long weekly team meeting, which is quite stressful as Sarah and a couple of other members of the team get into yet another mass debate about issues that can't be resolved at the current time. Sarah is openly 'bad-mouthing' her own manager about the way the department is being run and it isn't a very pleasant experience.

- At 1.00pm Dave and Sarah have their monthly 1:1 review (which hasn't been cancelled for a change). Sarah's mobile keeps ringing during the meeting and her comments infuriate Dave, as she is being critical and doesn't give him a chance to explain why things are the way they are. At the end of the meeting, Dave asks Sarah if he can talk about something personal, but she says there isn't time and tells him to speak to her at the end of the day.

- Sarah goes away from her desk at about 3.00pm. It looks like she has unexpectedly left early for the day, without giving Dave an opportunity to talk to her about his personal issue (whether he can have some time off for the funeral). Dave doesn't know where Sarah is, and now a customer is trying to urgently get hold of her and he doesn't know what to do.

Now let's rewind the clock and start the day again …

## Dave's day at the office – TAKE 2

- Dave found out that a relative had died unexpectedly last night, so he isn't feeling his normal self. As he comes in to work his manager Sarah looks up from her desk, smiles and in her usual friendly manner, says, 'Hi, how are you?' Dave lets her know about his bereavement and Sarah offers some kind words. She immediately lets him know that he can have compassionate leave for the funeral and says that if he's struggling to cope with his work today, or feels he needs to go home early, to let her know.

- Dave is relieved to see a relatively clean inbox when he turns on his computer. He does find an instruction to do a new piece of work from Sarah, but it's clearly explained and he thinks he can cope with it OK. He just needs to check one small piece of information with Sarah, and although she looks busy, when he checks, she is happy to answer his question.

- Dave is also pleased that Sarah replies promptly to an outstanding question via email and has given him the information that he needs in order to meet a deadline.

- At 11.30am Dave attends the weekly team meeting, which is scheduled for an hour but normally ends up being shorter. Sarah is good at keeping to a tight agenda, covering things clearly and succinctly. She is good at forewarning the team of issues that might affect them, and is good at getting them back on track if decisions can't be made immediately, preventing unnecessary debate. Sarah is very professional, and always talks with respect about other members of the team and department.

- At 1.00pm Sarah and Dave have their scheduled monthly 1:1 review, which Sarah always makes time for no matter how busy she is. During the 1:1 she is never distracted and always makes Dave feel important and valued. Sarah has a couple of problems to raise with Dave about his work. However, she listens to his point of view and they are jointly able to work out how to resolve the issues. Dave finds Sarah's feedback useful. Sarah makes time at the end of the meeting to talk to him about his bereavement and checks that he's OK to keep working.

- Sarah is called away unexpectedly at 3.00pm as her elderly mother has had a fall and has been taken to hospital. But as she leaves the office, she lets the team know why she's leaving and says that she will attempt to regularly check messages on her mobile phone.

Find ten differences between scenario 1 and 2, in the way Dave's manager communicates to him. (The answers are available at www.management-handbook.com)

How do you think that Dave would have felt at the end of the day in scenario 1 vs. scenario 2?

Linking back to Chapter A: 'Assessment', how do you think Dave would rate his manager in each scenario for the question: 'I think that my manager is a good manager'?

The point of this exercise is two-fold. Firstly, you would probably agree that Dave would be feeling far more positive about his manager in 'Take 2' versus 'Take 1', so you can see what an enormous difference good communication can make when compared to poor communication.

Secondly, it illustrates the critical point that communication affects virtually everything that we do at work, from how we interact with customers to how confident and competent people perceive us to be at our jobs. We communicate not only when we send an email or do a presentation – we are communicating all of the time, even when we don't think that we are. For example, whether you speak the words, 'Hi, how are you?' or simply stare at your computer looking stressed, you are sending a message to other people.

## Positively communicating

Here are eleven principles to help you ensure that your communications are at their best, summed up by our 'COMMUNICATE' acronym:

**C: Clarity**

*Give clear instructions so that people understand exactly what you are asking them to do for you.*

**O: Open**

*Maintain a warm and friendly body language and attitude, making people feel that you are approachable.*

**M: Make time**

*Make time for people who need to talk to you. If you are busy, politely agree upon a mutual time to reconvene and stick to it.*

**M: Maintain professionalism**

*Communicate professionally at all times, including through what you say, how you dress and the appearance of your work.*

**U: Updated**

*Where appropriate, keep people updated about where you are, what you are doing and why you are doing it.*

**N: Not all talk!**

*Practise two-way communication. Use this principle: you have two ears and one mouth, so use them in that ratio!*

## I: Informed (enough)

*Keep team members up to date on matters that are important and affect them, without bombarding them with too much detail.*

## C: Control

*Keep control over meetings you are running, avoiding going over and over issues or making inappropriate comments. Also keep control of your emotions.*

## A: Active interest

*Make people feel that you are focused on them when you are communicating with them, actively listening to them and not being distracted.*

## T: Timely

*Respond to people's requests for information and support in a timely manner and announce information at the appropriate time.*

## E: Expectations

*Manage people's expectations about when you will get back to them with information.*

---

How would applying these eleven principles have helped Sarah, the manager in 'Take 1'? How well do you COMMUNICATE?

- Give yourself a school report grade (A–F) for how good you are at demonstrating the eleven principles listed above.
- You may also wish to ask a close work colleague to give you feedback from their perspective. If you do, encourage them to be open and be accepting of their comments.

---

 We communicate all of the time, even when we aren't speaking. Managers need to ensure that their communications are helping, not hindering, their staff.

---

# D: Distributing work

*If my neighbour is happy, my own work will go easier, too.*
Macedonian proverb

Imagine that you've just been appointed as the head teacher of a school and that you encounter this scenario.

You've been promised by your predecessor that next year's timetable will be ready for you on your first day. To your great surprise, when you start your new job, you realize that the timetable consists of five ripped-up pieces of card with scrawled handwriting on them!

When you investigate how this timetable was created, you discover that the five pieces of card (one for each weekday) were placed in a room and the teachers (in a strict pecking order by subject, starting with the science department) were allowed to go in and choose whichever slots they wanted. It was apparent that the scientists didn't want to teach on Friday afternoons! The unfortunate teachers at the bottom of the pecking order then had the task of trying to cram their lessons into the remaining space. You also discover that a member of staff who should be working only three days per week has been forced to schedule her lessons over five days, and that one year group is entirely missing out on home economics, as the timetable simply doesn't allow it.

You have no choice but to go ahead with the old system of timetabling classes for the new intake of A-Level students, who are the senior pupils in the school and can choose whichever combination of subjects they would like to study. The old system involves telling them what slots are available and hoping that they can do the A-Level combination they want. Many of the students are annoyed because inflexibility in the timetable means that this isn't possible. You also realize that due to timetable clashes, the numbers in the A-Level classes are completely imbalanced. One Geography class has seventeen students, while another, taught by a different and very capable teacher, has just two.

The example above was in fact a real-life situation. Now answer the following questions:

---

**Distribution of work:**
- Why would some teachers be justifiably unhappy with their teaching timetable?
- What could you do differently next year to ensure that the workload was fairly spread?

**Procedure used to distribute work:**
- Why would some teachers be annoyed by the method used to distribute the work?
- What could you do differently next year to ensure that method of assigning the work was fair?

**Customer satisfaction:**
- How satisfied would your customers (i.e. the A-Level students) be with the system?

- What could you do differently to ensure a higher level of customer satisfaction?

---

When distributing work, you must ensure that the following things are achieved:

---

### Distributive justice

People need to feel that the distribution of work has been fair, in terms of the quantity, quality and schedule of when the work will take place. This is known as distributive justice.

This can be achieved by allowing the team members to divide up the workload between themselves, which works well if everyone in the team has an equal say and they can agree a solution that everyone is genuinely happy with.

Alternatively, the manager may need to fairly divide up the workload allocation on the team's behalf. In this situation it's extremely helpful if the manager asks the individual team members for their preferences (their 'must haves', 'nice to haves' and 'must not haves') based on their availability.

### Procedural justice

Procedural justice is when people can see that the method used to make a decision was fair. For example, people shouldn't think that their colleagues got a better deal just because they are their manager's friend (and we all know that happens).

To achieve procedural justice you should be transparent about the strategy used for workload allocation and you should be able to give a sound rationale for making any difficult decisions.

## Customer satisfaction

When at work it can be tempting to think: 'My job would be great … if I didn't have any customers.' But it's vital to remember that without customers you wouldn't have a job.

It's also useful for managers to remember that without team members, they wouldn't have a people management job. As a manager, you therefore have two groups of 'customers' to keep happy: the team's customers and your own team members. It's a manager's job to balance the needs of both parties.

In our school example, the real-life head teacher found it helpful to gather student preferences about what A-Level subjects they wanted to take, and teachers' preferences for when, where and who they wanted to teach; and then to try to juggle resources to meet everyone's needs. This was a better approach than the old system, where only employee preferences were taken into account.

## When you can't please everyone

It's impossible to please everyone all of the time. However, in this situation, it really helps if you are seen to do your very best to accommodate all of the 'must haves' and 'must not haves', and as many of the 'nice to haves' as is feasible. People will generally be understanding if not everything is possible and will be flexible in supporting you.

When it isn't possible to meet everyone's needs, next time ensure that the people who previously missed out are top priority to get what they want, and that the same people don't miss out again and again.

## Day-to-day management of workflow

A head teacher allocates teaching duties on an annual basis; other managers may have to allocate workload on a monthly, daily or even hourly basis. Regardless of how frequently this arises, the principles discussed above remain valid.

After you have allocated work, you will also be confronted by events that test the plan you have put in place. This could be anything from extra customer demand to unavailability of staff members (i.e. due to illness) or team member changes, which result in a mismatch between the work output required and the skill-set available.

As a manager, you are ultimately responsible for navigating through these obstacles. So, how best can you use the available resources to meet these challenges?

## Monitor workloads and redistribute where required

As a manager, it's vital that you keep a regular dialogue with all members of the team about their workloads. The people actually doing the work often spot problems and bottlenecks first. However, it's not normally within a team member's remit to redistribute work, and this needs to be done by the manager.

---

 A manager of two teams, Yvonne, was particularly bad at redistributing work. One of her teams was regularly working long hours while the other team (with a very similar skill-set) had much less work and were 'twiddling their thumbs'. Despite hearing the needs of the busy team who asked for extra help, Yvonne did nothing. It was only when confident members of the other team regularly saw the long hours being put in that they directly offered much-needed help to the busy team. Busy team members may not always be fortunate enough to have such proactive and compassionate colleagues.

This example is what teamwork is all about, and the manager should be at the forefront of that process, not at the end of it. Where there's more demand than can be managed by the people assigned to it, it's in the interests of the organization for additional resources to be drafted in. In this example the net cost of one team assisting another was zero. But it made a world of difference to the team under huge pressure, who were able to keep motivated and focus their efforts on producing good quality for their clients.

## Prioritize what to do first

Sometimes there's simply too much work to complete at once, therefore managers need to be able to decide what tasks should be completed first. You can use the following three criteria to help you gauge the priority of each task:

- **Necessity** – is the item of work something that *must* be completed at some point in time?
- **Urgency** – how quickly must this item of work be completed?
- **Value** – how much value does completing this task add in relation to other tasks you could do? (Note that higher-valued tasks are normally highly aligned with individual, team or organizational objectives.)

 Encourage your team to:
- Do high-value, urgent tasks first.
- Consider whether they need to prioritize high-value, non-urgent tasks over low-value, urgent ones.
- Regularly schedule time to do low-value, low-urgency tasks that they nevertheless *have* to do (such as mandatory training), otherwise they may never get done.

## Matching skill demand and supply

Let's imagine you have two people in your team available to take on work: person A is highly experienced, person B is a junior with much less experience. One Monday you receive two items of work, one each from client X and client Y. Both are equally valuable, urgent and necessary. Do you assign one piece to person A and one piece to person B?

Just as you can prioritize according to value, urgency and necessity, you can use another criterion, task difficulty, to help you assign tasks. For example, when you review the work required, you find that client X's is straightforward and easy, while client Y's is complex and intense. Given that you want to achieve the best outcome in quality in the time available, you wouldn't want to assign person B, the junior member of the team, to the complex request from client Y. When using this criterion to allocate work, make sure that you also take time to develop the less experienced individual, for example, by walking them through how the complex work task was completed, at a less busy time.

---

Pull together a list of your recent or current workload.

- How well was the workload shared among the team?
- Rate whether the items were necessary, and how urgent and valuable they were.

- Was the right person from your team assigned to each item, so that you got the best outcome possible?

What do you learn from doing this that you can apply to workload that you will need to distribute in the future?

 Allocate workload fairly, then monitor how well the workload is being completed, making adjustments where necessary.

# E: Empowerment

*In most cases being a good boss means hiring talented people and then getting out of their way.*

Tina Fey

Julie is an intelligent, diligent, well-qualified, enthusiastic and capable employee with over eight years of experience in her profession. Yet her manager insists on knowing virtually *every detail* of her work, overseeing almost *every decision* and 'clock watching' her even though she works many hours of overtime. Julie's manager deliberately listens in on her conversations and then frequently butts in with her unwelcome opinion, so now Julie makes phone calls only when her manager isn't there! The whole situation is driving Julie insane and she's contemplating leaving what would otherwise be a great job.

Julie certainly isn't the only person to feel like she's being 'micro-managed'. Our equally capable friend Nick told us that he's required to get approval from his manager before sending *any* email, either externally or internally.

Julie and Nick could both benefit from being managed in a more empowered way. So what actually is 'empowerment'?

**KEY TERM**

**Empowerment** is where employees are given the responsibility for making decisions about their own work. These decisions can be small or large depending on the level of empowerment that a manager wants to give, and may include:

- What work they do (e.g. employees are free to manage their own workload/diary).
- Where they work (e.g. working from home instead of the office).
- When they work (e.g. the ability to work flexible hours).
- How they complete their work (e.g. how they structure information in a presentation).

**THINK ABOUT IT**

What are the benefits of having an empowering management style:

- For the employee?
- For the manager?
- For the organization?
- For the customer?

My experience of working for a manager, called Chris, who had an empowering style was very positive. It was time-efficient, as I knew what I needed to do and I could just get on and do it. I felt that my ideas, efforts and opinions were valued. I enjoyed being given the freedom to work the way that I wanted to work and I genuinely believe that it brought out the best in me. Hopefully you can identify with having had this kind of experience too.

Chris shared with me what influenced him to manage in this way.

---

About twenty years ago, Chris did a job that required him to write reports. His manager wanted to approve them before they were sent to customers and inevitably his work would, rather demoralizingly, come back covered in red pen showing numerous corrections. The reports would often need to be reworked several times, with the manager even changing his own corrections.

Over time, Chris identified that his manager was correcting his style and not the actual content of his work. Interestingly, when his manager was away on holiday, Chris's work was approved without the need for corrections by a deputy manager who was happy with it, as were Chris's customers.

Chris realized that people have their own personal styles and one person's opinion of 'good' can be another person's opinion of 'bad'. Although it's vital to correct clearly inappropriate style or errors, Chris now believes that if the content is satisfactory you should avoid demotivating people by forcing them to do things your way. A manager's decision or method isn't necessarily the *right* or the *only* way to do something.

---

It's very apparent how this experience has translated to Chris's own management style. Chris gives a clear outline of the 'must have' criteria he needs from his team members and then lets them 'run with it', knowing that as long as they meet these expectations, they can make their own decisions about how to do so. And crucially, having been given this freedom, when their work is reviewed, Chris is very accepting of the decisions his employees have made, only correcting things that will really make a difference. His main focus is on asking the question, 'Will our customers be satisfied?', and most of the time the answer is yes. On the few occasions when this isn't the case, Chris has more time to spend recovering the situation, as he isn't micromanaging or involved in constant, unnecessary reworking.

It's always worth remembering the **80:20 principle**: that 80% of the benefit is created from 20% of the work. As a manager, your job is to identify the 20% of decisions that will really make the difference and focus efforts on that, rather than constantly trying to change the 80% of things that aren't worth it and demoralizing your staff in the process.

## Creating an empowered environment

Here are some practical ways to create an empowered environment, summed up using our 'EMPOWER' acronym:

## E: Expectations

*Set clear expectations, defining what is needed, by when, and outline any 'must have' criteria. Also agree expectations of when you will meet to review progress.*

## M: My responsibility

*Set clear boundaries, ensuring that employees understand what falls within their boundary of responsibility to do and make decisions on.*

## P: Pareto principle

*This is also known as the 80:20 rule, i.e. you should look for the 20% of decisions that will make 80% of the difference and give people freedom with the other 80%.*

## O: Open and approachable

*Make yourself accessible for when people need support. If things go wrong, ensure that your team feel that you are approachable and that you work together to resolve the issue. Create a no-blame culture and help people to learn from their mistakes.*

## W: What (not how)

*Understand that people will perform best if they are given the freedom to work the way they want to work, and remember that it's the output that matters. For example, if someone does their best work while listening to music through headphones, let them do it unless there's a valid reason not to.*

### E: Encourage knowledge-sharing

*The more informed people are, the better the decisions they can make. If you create a culture where staff will inform their manager about the decisions they take, the manager can take action in the event that the decision was inappropriate.*

### R: Risk-assess

*Teach people to risk-assess their decisions. Before making a decision on their own, team members should consider whether this decision will have any legal, safety, reputational or financial implications if they get it wrong. If not, this is a rule of thumb that your staff can make the decision on their own.*

## Should you empower people ALL of the time?

Part of being good at empowering people is knowing when it's appropriate to do it and when it isn't. Look at the following grid, which is based on the work of Paul Hersey and Ken Blanchard, and identify which quadrant Julie (from the start of the chapter) would fall into.

Hopefully you have placed Julie in the '**High will, High skill**' category. When people like Julie are capable and motivated they are likely to thrive in an empowered culture.

---

If someone falls into the '**High will, Low skill**' category, empowering them can be less easy, but it isn't impossible.

For example, James manages graduate trainees on a rotation scheme where they will work for several months at a time in different departments. This means that when a new trainee arrives, however enthusiastic they are, they would be very unlikely to be able to do the skilled, technical work that the team performs. In this situation, James still tries to empower these people by giving the opportunity to have a go. However, he manages their expectations that they might not get it right first time, but that's fine because they will learn from their mistakes. He also builds their confidence because they will at least have tried, even if amendments are required – and this still will be better than James having to do it all himself.

---

When someone falls into the '**Low will, High skill**' category, empowering them can be difficult, because empowerment requires confidence that a person will deliver what you need them to do. Before empowering such an individual, managers should try to find out what is causing their lack of motivation and address it wherever possible. Remember that empowerment can be a great way to motivate people, for example by giving them opportunities to try new work. If you have empowered someone in this category, it's important to agree (and stick to) reasonable milestones for monitoring progress, to ensure that they are on track.

Finally, when someone falls into the '**Low will, Low skill**' category, although empowerment is something to aim for longer term, it probably isn't immediately the right solution. If a person isn't capable of doing the work and has no desire to try, then empowerment won't be helpful to either them or their manager. Probably the first step is to try to understand what is causing the lack of motivation and address this, as it can be difficult to improve someone's skill if they aren't motivated.

## Can you give someone too much empowerment?

Yes! For example, Penny has asked her manager time and time again what she is meant to be doing and keeps being told just to go away and work it out for herself. While empowerment is generally good, too much empowerment can be a bad thing.

It's crucial to note that empowerment does *not* mean that a manager can devolve his or her responsibility for management. Even the most motivated and capable employees need management.

---

 Empowerment can bring workplace satisfaction for both employee and manager. Managers should empower on a case-by-case basis, depending on the person's **skill** and **will**.

---

# F: Feedback

*Feedback is the breakfast of champions.*
Ken Blanchard

During a management training course we divided a group of people into three teams. One member of each team was blindfolded and was given the task of throwing ten bean-bags into a waste paper bin, aiming to get as many in as they could. Unbeknown to the blindfolded people, the rest of their teams had been briefed:

- Team 1 were only allowed to make feedback-neutral statements (e.g. 'Here's a beanbag.')
- Team 2 had the same condition as Team 1, with the addition that they could give positive feedback and encouragement to the person (e.g. 'You've got that one in, well done.')
- Team 3 had the same conditions as Team 2, with the addition that they could also give the blindfolded person suggestions for improvement (e.g. 'You just needed to throw that one a little bit further.')

**THINK ABOUT IT** Which team do you think got the highest number of beanbags in the bin? Do you think there's any difference in how the blindfolded people felt while doing the task? If so, why?

On completing the task, we asked each of the blindfolded people how they felt during the exercise.

The thrower in Team 1 said that he understood what he had to do, but quickly got frustrated because he didn't know whether his efforts were paying off, or if there was anything that he could do to improve. It was more irritating because he could hear the other throwers being told whether they had hit or missed, yet he didn't have a clue how he was doing.

Team 2 did marginally better than Team 1. The thrower in Team 2 said that she liked the encouragement at first; it made her feel motivated and getting feedback on whether she was on target was useful. She also commented, however, that she found the task difficult because the only way that she could improve was to try to work it out for herself, which was hard. She also found the encouragement patronizing towards the end because her team members were constantly saying she could do it, when it was clear to her that she couldn't.

Team 3 did significantly better than both of the other teams. The thrower liked the encouragement and the feedback on his performance. He found it useful to know where he was going wrong when he missed, he really enjoyed the task and liked the challenge of trying to improve, and he enjoyed being the winner.

We hope that you can see why this is such a powerful example of why it's good to have:

- An appropriate amount of encouragement.
- Clear instructions about what output you are expecting from someone.
- A way to give feedback to someone so that they know when they have successfully achieved what was expected of them.
- Feedback on how they can perform even better.

In the next chapter, G: 'Goal Setting', we give guidance on how to set objectives against which you can give feedback.

## But people don't like receiving negative feedback ...

If people in your team find developmental feedback hard to accept, you might like to try the beanbag exercise with them, as it's a really useful technique to explain why both **positive** and **developmental** feedback is beneficial to you.

 If people describe your feedback as 'negative' – and more importantly, come away feeling that way – perhaps this is also a sign that you could have delivered the message better.

## How to deliver 'negative' feedback in a positive way

Laura explained that her manager was required to give her some developmental feedback on behalf of a more senior manager. Laura said she could clearly see that the feedback wasn't positive and that she had areas where she needed to improve. The key message was that she needed to demonstrate more control over her emotions at work. Some managers might cringe at the thought of having to deliver this type of message, accurately seeing the potential for the person to take the feedback very personally and walk away from the discussion feeling (ironically) very emotional.

Yet Laura said that she left the meeting feeling really good about the feedback and highly motivated by it. So what was the secret of this manager's feedback success?

Looking back, Laura realized that her manager had taken time out to consider what was important to her (she wanted to achieve a promotion) and he had cleverly used this as a hook, to help her see the benefits to her of trying to improve in this area.

---

 Obviously if you're looking for a motivational 'hook' it's important to use the hook sincerely, so make sure that there's a genuine link between a change in the target area and the person's desired goal.

When giving someone developmental feedback always look for the WIIFM factor – which stands for 'What's in it for me?' – and try to tap into it.

---

# How to give development feedback without making a person defensive

A very helpful way to give difficult feedback without making a person defensive is to use a psychological self-identification technique called 'You, Me, Agree'.

**YOU:** The first step is focused on trying to get the person to self-identify the feedback that you need to give them. For example, in Laura's case, this might involve asking her:

- What an effective level of emotional control looks like in the workplace.
- How she sees herself against the benchmark of the 'good' level that she has just set.
- How she can close the gap between where she is now and the benchmark that she has just set.

**ME:** Next confirm that the standard she has proposed would be a useful way to behave, adding any other feedback such as helpful suggestions for improvement.

**AGREE:** Your aim by the end of the discussion is to have a shared understanding of what 'good' looks like, how the person is performing or behaving currently, and what they might do to improve in future.

Why do people sometimes get defensive when they are simply told that they need to improve? Why is it helpful to use self-identification while giving feedback?

## When should I give feedback?

A great rule of thumb for managers is that they should never give feedback to a person in their annual performance review that they haven't already heard before. If people are surprised with your feedback, you haven't communicated well enough with them during the year.

## But why is timely feedback important?

Let's look back to our beanbag-throwing exercise. How useful would it be to the throwers to get feedback on how they could have improved their performance three months after the task? Absolutely useless. Our memories decay with time, plus we've had three months of potentially doing the task over and over again (making the same mistakes) in the meantime.

We aren't saying that you need to jump on a person's back every time there's something you have feedback on, but if you do have useful comments, they are best delivered sooner rather than later. Plus this demonstrates that you are actually interested in how someone is doing, and that their performance is important.

# If there's nothing but positive things to say ...

Finally, let's imagine that it's the first time your blindfolded thrower has managed to get all ten beanbags into the bin. He's been practising, and all that hard work has paid off. He'd probably feel justifiably delighted with his performance.

Now let's imagine that you ask him to keep going. He subsequently improves so much that he can throw all ten beanbags into the bin every time he attempts it. Congratulations, didn't he do well!

But does this work excite and motivate him any more? Probably not. He can do it without even trying, and you can envisage a situation whereby he would start getting a bit sloppy because he doesn't need to concentrate as hard as he used to in order to succeed.

Humans have a natural desire to get better and better. When you can juggle with three balls, then you enjoy trying with four; when you can complete the easy level on a video game you get hooked on trying to master progressively harder levels. So when someone is doing their job so well, to the point that they are getting great results every time, this is feedback to you to check that your team member is sufficiently challenged. If someone can metaphorically 'do their job with their eyes shut', then over time they may become bored and demotivated and their standards can slip as a result.

Crucially, if you do make a person's job harder to keep them challenged, make sure that they see this change as a positive step. There's a big difference between:

A. Doing twice as much work as everyone else in the same time;

and

B. Being given a new and exciting project that will stretch and grow you.

---

Timely feedback is vital to keep your team motivated, performing at their best, and delivering what you've agreed you expect from them.

---

# G: Goal-setting

*Management by objectives works if you first think through your objectives. Ninety percent of the time you haven't.*

Peter Drucker

Goals (or objectives) are normally set as part of a formal performance appraisal process. Typical management text-books will often cite a range of reasons for doing performance reviews and setting goals, for example:

- To monitor performance against what is expected.

- To motivate staff to work to achieve specific important things.

- To identify and fill any training needs.

- To recognize staff who have achieved their goals, often linking to financial reward.

- To support individuals to work towards their own career aspirations.

It all sounds great in theory. A date will be fixed once or twice a year when managers and employees officially sit down together and discuss all of these important things. Time well spent.

But how often is it *actually* time well spent?

- Have you ever felt that performance reviews are a complete pain and that you're just going through the motions?

- Have you ever not bothered to look at your objectives until the week before your annual performance review, at which point you have to conjure up evidence to show that you've been working towards them all year?

- How frequently could you accurately describe what your current objectives are, without looking at them? (That shows how focused we are on the goals we have been set.)

- Have you ever felt cynical that it doesn't really matter how well you meet your objectives, because in reality other factors really determine promotions and pay rises?

Sometimes appraisals do reap the benefits listed above. Our friend Rachel commented that she comes out of her performance appraisals feeling really motivated, both about the progress that she has made, and to achieve future goals. So how can managers help everyone to feel like Rachel and conduct the appraisal system in a way that really adds value?

# Seven steps to objective-setting

Here are seven practical steps to setting goals that motivate people and drive the performance that organizations need. We will illustrate the steps using the example of Adam, who is a secondary school teacher.

## Step 1: Find out what reward an individual is incentivized to achieve

- Adam's manager asks what he wants to achieve over the next review period, and Adam says that he's really motivated to try to achieve a 'top performers' bonus this year.

## Step 2: Clarify what needs to be achieved to receive this reward

- To be classified as a top performer in Adam's organization, he needs to 'exceed expectations' against all of his performance objectives.

## Step 3: Work out which areas of the job role should have objectives set against them

- Adam and his manager review his job description, which summarizes the ten main duties of Adam's role. Six of his duties are strongly linked to the success of the students and therefore the school (e.g. teaching lessons, marking homework and grading exam papers). The other four duties are less 'business-critical' (e.g. dressing the classroom environment). Adam and his manager therefore agree to set objectives around the six most critical areas.

## Step 4: Agree performance objectives against the important areas of the role

- For each of the six business-critical areas, Adam and his manager agree what acceptable performance looks like. They then write objectives for each area, ensuring that they are specific, measurable and time-bound.
- *For example, with regard to the duty of marking exam papers, acceptable performance might be: Marking and returning 100% of student exam papers within two weeks of the students sitting the exams, and passing the school's verification check that the exam papers have been marked to an acceptable standard.*

## Step 5. Ensure that the employee is given examples of what performance would be rated as failing to meet the objective and exceeding expectations

- When defining 'exceeding expectations', you don't have to precisely outline what performance must occur, as it's difficult to predict the unknown, but you should give examples of what is good enough to 'exceed expectations' of performance.
- *For example, for Adam to 'exceed expectations' with regard to his marking objective, marking a whole extra class's exam papers may be sufficient to achieve this*

*rating, but marking just one additional paper may not be enough.*

## Step 6: Regular monitoring of performance against the objectives, providing ongoing support to maximize the employee's ability to meet the objectives

- Employees and their managers should have regular 1:1 meetings to discuss their performance. This is an ideal opportunity to revisit objectives (and review whether they are on track to achieve them or not) and identify any knowledge/skills gaps and how to address them.

- *For example, Adam may be concerned that exams are approaching next month and he is feeling unconfident about his ability to mark papers accurately and consistently. Therefore it may be helpful to receive additional training.*

## Step 7: Carry out a formal appraisal and provide the reward as agreed if achieved

- During the review, you should look back and evaluate previous progress against the objectives set, and repeat the process again for the next review period.

- *If employees have failed to meet their objectives (and there are no extenuating circumstances) then ask yourself what more you could have done to help them to succeed.*

**THINK ABOUT IT**

Why is it helpful to give people who do the same job a set of core identical performance objectives?

One of your answers to the above question may that it's easier to compare how well people have performed (e.g. if allocating a bonus) if people have been measured against the same criteria. Another may have been that when you use the seven steps to objective-setting, managers are focused on setting goals around the most business-critical aspects of the role.

In addition to standard ('core') objectives, managers can also set and agree some additional objectives that are unique to the individual.

Let's imagine that someone is aiming to be promoted to the next level in their job (Step 1: Identifying reward). It may be agreed, as per Step 2 (Requirements to merit the reward), that the individual needs to meet or exceed all core objectives in their current role, plus meet some additional set objectives from the next level above.

## Setting objectives that drive the desired behaviour

This process aims to set objectives around aspects of performance that really makes a difference to customers and therefore the success of the organization. Linking back to Adam and our school example, although dressing the classroom might have positive effects for the students, if an objective is set only around this, and not around the things that really matter (e.g. teaching high-quality lessons), then it can drive teachers to put undue emphasis on this less important aspect of the job, as this is what is being measured.

What is being measured drives the performance you get, so when setting goals, it's important to design them around the behaviour or performance that you really need to see.

Using a different example, in a call centre, people may be set objectives around answering the phone within a set number of rings or taking a certain number of calls per hour. However, this can drive behaviour that wasn't intended. Employees may pick up the telephone receiver within three rings and then put it down again. A better measure would be to monitor the number of customer enquiries that can be resolved to a satisfactory standard by the individual who answers the call.

Organizational success should be aligned with the achievement of each individual's goals, which must be specific and measurable.

# H: Hiring

*Time spent on hiring is time well spent.*

Robert Half

Jon was being interviewed for a role at a different company. The receptionist asked him to go through to the interview room, and as he entered he saw that the interviewer was sitting with his feet on the desk, reading a newspaper. Continuing to read the paper, the interviewer said: 'Hello Jonathan, why are you here and what the f*** do you want from me?' These were the only two questions that Jon was asked throughout the entire interview, with the interviewer doing the rest of the talking. Jon was not offered the job.

---

You can judge for yourself, on a scale of 1 (appalling) to 5 (outstanding), how well Jon's interviewer did against the following criteria that should be met when selecting employees:

1. Selection of the candidate most likely to perform well in the position.
2. Creation of a positive impression of the organization for the candidates.
3. Fairness, ensuring that selection methods are used ethically and are not unfairly biased against certain groups of people (e.g. disabled people).

---

## What are you aiming for during employee selection?

It's genuinely quite shocking how bad some managers can be when recruiting. We've learnt that senior managers in an international finance organization are interviewed using the question: 'So what's your favourite film?' And middle (female) managers are asked: 'So when do you intend to have children?' Both of these interview questions are totally inappropriate, the first because it's irrelevant to success in the role. The second question is considered potentially discriminatory against women.

This chapter therefore gives you a seven-step guide to hiring.

### Step 1: Business case

Ensure that there is a business case to hire a new employee, determining:

- Is recruitment of additional labour necessary?
- If so, what is the basic purpose of the job?
- How many hours of employee labour are required per week/month/year?
- How long you will require labour for?
- What budget is available to finance the position?
- On what basis do you want to employ the individual, e.g. permanent; contract; job-share, etc.?

Where appropriate, you should get sign-off from a suitable person in your organization to begin the recruitment process, e.g. your manager or Human Resources (HR).

## Step 2: Job description

You will need to source or create an accurate job description for the role you are recruiting for. A job description states (in writing):

- The **job title**.
- The **purpose** of the job.
- How the job fits into the **organization structure** (including specification of who will manage the employee and any job roles the employee will manage).
- The **physical location** of the job.
- A list of the **key tasks or duties** to be performed.
- An overview of the **key accountabilities**, i.e. the things that the job holder will be responsible for.
- **Any unusual requirements** (e.g. the need to be on-call outside of standard working hours).

If you have never prepared a job description before, it's recommended that you seek additional help doing this, such as from an HR advisor. If the role already exists, you can use an existing job description, ensuring that it's accurate for the current role. Job descriptions should be written in clear, straightforward and non-discriminatory language (e.g. they should be gender-neutral).

## Step 3: Person specification (selection criteria)

Next, you need to identify the attributes that a person should have in order to carry out the job, as defined in the job description. This can be structured using the following headings:

- **Educational and professional qualifications** – stating the minimum level of acceptable qualification.
- **Competencies** – transferrable skills (e.g. time management; written communication; oral communication; creativity, customer focus, etc.).
- **Experience** – listing tasks specific to the job at hand (e.g. for a PR role, experience writing press releases).
- **Personal characteristics** – this can include essential physical requirements (e.g. the ability to lift a certain amount of weight, but only if it's essential to the job; and by including this, you should not automatically disqualify certain groups, such as women or people with disabilities).

It's critical that all of the criteria listed are directly relevant to the position, and you must be able to justify that they are necessary in order to successfully perform the role.

It's useful to classify your criteria into 'essential' and 'desirable'. People who do not have 'essential' criteria should be ruled out straight away, so make sure that anything classified in this way is *actually* essential, as you will be ruling out otherwise excellent candidates who do not meet these criteria. Desirable criteria can help you to choose among candidates who meet all of the essential criteria.

## Step 4: Open the application process to candidates

There are many ways to source candidates, including internal vacancy boards; job adverts in newspapers; job centres; online recruitment; recruitment agencies; recruitment fairs; referrals from existing staff members. The best method to use depends on the position you're hiring for, whether it's a skilled or unskilled role, and whether the candidate needs experience (i.e. must have a specific degree). In some cases it's better to use multiple avenues to get a better pool of candidates rather than rely upon one alone.

When advertising the role, you will need to specify how you want candidates to apply (e.g. by completing an application form or submitting a CV (résumé) with covering letter).

Relevant questions to ask on an application form could include:

- Name, address, telephone numbers and email address of candidate.
- Educational and professional qualifications.
- Work experience.
- Names and addresses of referees.

You may wish to include some initial screening or competency-based questions, to test for essential criteria. Be careful to avoid possible discriminatory questions (e.g. asking them to indicate if they have childcare responsibilities).

## Step 5: Draw up a shortlist

Review all of the applications against the person specification, and rule out any candidates who do not meet any of the essential criteria. Where you are unable to progress all remaining candidates to the next stage of the selection process, use the desirable criteria to choose between applicants. Do not exclude people from progressing to the next stage upon the basis of their membership of a certain group (i.e. do not exclude women because you think that they may soon start a family, even if you are hoping to find someone who will fill the role for a number of years).

---

 For a shortlist to be worthwhile it's advisable to have no fewer than three candidates, ideally five. You may wish to have more than one person involved in drawing up the shortlist, to try to overcome the issue of biased selection.

---

Once you have a shortlist, invite the successful applicants to the next stage of the selection process, giving them clear details about when and where it will take place, what will happen at the next stage, and anything specific that they need to do to prepare for it. Where applicable, you should give directions on how to get to the venue and inform them who to ask for upon arrival. You should also ask candidates to inform you of any special requirements they have during the selection process (e.g. if they require wheelchair access); however, this information must not influence the selection decision.

## Step 6: Assess applicants

There are many different ways of assessing applicants. Here are some guidelines about three commonly used methods:

**Interviews**: You can use a structured or unstructured method. A structured interview is where you ask the same questions to every candidate, deliberately probing the areas detailed as essential or desirable in the person specification. In the unstructured format, the interviewer is free to ask whatever question he or she chooses and the process may therefore vary between candidates. Research has clearly shown that the structured interview process leads to better and fairer outcomes. They are superior at predicting who is likely to perform better in the role, and fairer because the interview is assessing only criteria known to be linked to success in the role (rather than a person's favourite film for a finance management role!).

**Work samples**: This is where you ask candidates to perform a sample of the actual job. For example, a teacher may be asked to design and teach a lesson. Work samples are one of the best ways of predicting who is likely to perform well in a role, since candidates are doing part of the actual job. They are also typically considered to be a fair selection method, since the assessment mirrors the actual job. When using work samples, it's useful to sample as many of the most important aspects of the job as is practical, and avoid placing too much emphasis on sampling infrequent or relatively unimportant aspects of the position.

**Psychometric tests**: Sometimes ability and personality tests are used to support selection decisions. These methods, when used properly, can give valuable information about how suitable a candidate is for a job. However, when using these methods, it's critical that managers work with someone who is qualified to select an appropriate test, administer and score it, and understand how test scores relate to whether to offer a candidate a job.

During the selection process it's useful to:
- Put candidates at ease and welcome them.
- Introduce any assessors and explain the structure of the assessment.
- Give the candidate an opportunity to ask questions.
- Keep candidates informed about what will happen next.
- Make detailed notes about what happened during the selection process; however, only record what you

observed or heard (not what you think of the candidate, as this is an opinion, not fact).
- Thank the candidate for their time.
- Have more than one person present, to share the burden of work (e.g. one person takes notes, while the other asks questions) and to make decision-making fairer by having more than one person's opinion.

## Step 7: Make a decision and communicate it

The final stage of the selection process is to make a decision about who to offer the job to and which candidates to reject. This should be linked clearly to the essential and desirable criteria listed in the person specification. Sometimes hiring managers use a formal scoring system, other times they don't; however, it's useful to record a summary of your decision-making on a single sheet, in case your recruitment decision is challenged. Always keep records relating to selection decisions confidential and securely stored.

It's very important to candidates that you communicate the outcome of selection decisions as quickly as possible, even if the candidate has not been successful. They will have invested time in your recruitment process and may be very keen to be offered the job, or may be choosing between multiple offers. Where a delay is unavoidable, keep them updated as to when they will hear more news. If unsuccessful candidates ask for feedback, you can explain how they differed from the successful candidate in terms of essential and desirable criteria.

Once you have offered the successful candidate a job, there are two types of offer. Firstly, a conditional offer, which means that the job offer is subject to various conditions, e.g. receipt of satisfactory references or proof of qualifications. Secondly, unconditional, which means that no further criteria need to be satisfied before the offer is final.

---

- Imagine you are recruiting for your own role. Have a go at planning how you would go about applying the seven steps to hiring to select a suitable candidate, in a fair manner.
- Think back to how you were actually recruited into your job. How well did you manager follow the seven steps?

---

We hope that this guide gives a useful overview of how to hire individuals into your team. Remember that, where applicable, you should always check with your manager or HR team to understand the specific policies and procedures for your own organization (for example, who makes the job offer).

---

Your employees are one of the greatest assets your organization will have – if not *the* greatest. Therefore a manager must always aim to hire the right person – someone with the necessary qualifications, competencies, experience and personal characteristics.

---

# I: Induction

*You never get a second chance to make a first impression.*
Will Rogers

You've chosen the candidate who you would like to join your team, so now come the formalities. Assuming that they have accepted the offer verbally, the next stage will be to send out an offer letter. This may be sent on your behalf – for example, by the HR department – and will typically include:

- The employee's name
- The job title
- Any conditions on which the job is offered (e.g. receipt of satisfactory references)
- The proposed date that employment will commence
- Confirmation of any actions that the employee needs to take prior to, or on day one of the role
- A reference to attached terms and conditions of employment.

The new employee is likely to be required to return a signed copy of the letter to the organization. Where the job has been offered conditionally and those conditions have been satisfied, your organization should also send a second letter to inform the individual that the job offer is now unconditional.

**CASE STUDY**

Sally told us of the story of one candidate who was perfect for the role – had the right experience, right people skills, right technical abilities. The one thing that he didn't have was the right grades on his résumé. So when the employer performed a rigorous background check, the candidate failed and the job offer was withdrawn, just weeks before he was due to start. With no back-up candidate left, Sally and her team were left in the lurch during a very busy time and had to go back to square one. It's always best to be prepared for this to happen.

## What about the less formal things that managers can do?

Anna raves about her manager. Their working relationship got off to a great start before Anna even joined the organization. Here's what happened. Anna's manager Joe was not on the interview panel and therefore had not met her during the selection process. When she was offered the job he contacted her, introducing himself and saying that it would be great to meet her before she started. Since Anna was relocating from a place that was a four-hour drive away, Joe realized that she would be house-hunting. He therefore sent her details of possible properties to rent and recommended areas to live in. Joe and Anna met for coffee when she was in the area to view a future house. And this was just the beginning. On day one in the role, Joe met Anna at reception, showed her everything and introduced her to loads of people. This gave Anna some useful knowledge and contacts, and left her with a really positive impression of her manager, which has never faded since.

---

**What's interesting** about Anna's story is that the amount of time and effort that Joe put in to supporting Anna was actually relatively light. It didn't take him much time to send her property particulars, make recommendations using local knowledge or meet her for coffee. Yet the impact that it had on Anna was really positive. Sometimes a little investment of your time creating the 'wow' factor for a new employee can reap dividends.

---

## Inductions don't always go so well

When starting to write this chapter, I thought it might be helpful to glance through a folder I was given when I started a new job aged 23, rather cheesily entitled: 'Employee Induction Pack – "Our Way of Working"'. If I'm completely honest, today is the first time I have ever looked through this folder. Since I consider myself to be normally a very diligent person, it left me wondering: how many of my fellow new recruits read all 52 pages of small print, completed the well-intentioned activities, received a certificate from their manager and sent a copy of it to HR as requested?

This absolutely crucial phase in my employee lifecycle was wasted. They say that first impressions count, and research shows that this really is true when it comes to employee induction.

---

**CASE STUDY**

Some companies induct employees into their organization really well. But this certainly doesn't always happen. Take Gary, for example, who was hired by a senior manager while his actual line manager was away on holiday. Gary started his job on the day that she returned from holiday, and she didn't speak to him for three days – until she eventually asked him who on earth he was! Things went from bad to worse. When Gary asked her what work he should do, she told him that he'd better go and organize his own work, because it wouldn't appear out of thin air, as if by magic! It eventually took Gary over a month to organize his own access to the basic computer systems he needed to do his job. That's clearly how not to do it.

---

## So how do you give someone a sound induction?

Rather than providing you with 52 pages of small print, let's keep it simple. There are nine key things that employees need as soon as possible after starting a new job, which are summed up by our 'INDUCTION' acronym:

**I: Importance of job**

Inform the employee how their job is connected to the overall success of the organization and why their role is important.

**N: Necessary tools and resources**

Provide access to all the tools and resources that the employee needs in order to complete their work and function in their new working environment.

**D: Duties**

Ensure that the employee understands what work they are there to complete, what is expected of them, and how their progress will be measured (i.e. set clear objectives).

**U: Understand how to complete the work**

As well as ensuring that the employee knows what to do, they also need to be confident that they know how to do it. This may require identifying skills and knowledge gaps and taking action to fill them.

**C: Communicate the organization's vision and strategy**

Ensure that the employee understands the purpose of the organization and the strategy that is being used to achieve this.

**T: Team**

Explain the structure of the organization and the purpose of each of the major divisions, giving more detail about your own team/division.

### I: Introductions

*Introduce the employee to other members of the team and to key contacts.*

### O: Organizational policies and procedures

*Inform employees of critical organizational policies and procedures (such as what to do in the event of a fire alarm) and give them the opportunity to familiarize themselves with less critical policies.*

### N: Now!

*Give them work to do as early as possible in their role. Don't leave them hanging around with nothing to do.*

---

- How well did your organization/manager do this 'Induction' checklist when you joined your current organization? Give each of the nine areas a school report grade from A–F.
- Why are each of the nine areas so important?

---

Some organizations have a formal induction programme to welcome new starters into the organization, covering some of the points listed above. Where this is the case, make sure that the employee attends the session as soon as possible after starting their new role. It's rather pointless to send someone on the induction course several months after they joined.

Where components are not covered by a company induction programme, or that information cannot be provided in a timely enough fashion, managers must take responsibility for ensuring that all of the material covered in the induction checklist is delivered to individuals as soon as is practically possible after they start their new role.

---

 Inductions can add a lot of value if done properly. Give new employees a good first impression of the organization and help them to feel like they're part of the family early on.

---

# J: Justice

*Fairness is not an attitude. It's a professional skill that must be developed and exercised.*

Brit Hume

My schoolteacher once told me that her daughter had a tantrum because she was given a smaller piece of cake than her sister. So from that point onwards my teacher devised a new strategy: one child would cut the cake and then the other child had to choose which piece she wanted. Funnily enough, there were never any more cake squabbles after that. The system was fair.

It would seem that fair treatment is important to us during childhood, and while most of us don't have tantrums in the office (at least, we hope not!), the need to be treated justly in comparison to others certainly stays with us into adulthood.

What is particularly fascinating is just how irritating being treated unfairly at work can be. And we aren't really focusing on the big things like pay here. It's often the little things that can really get under our skin.

How come some people manage to get away with doing far fewer hours than others – late starts, long lunches, early finishes and tea breaks in between? And have you noticed that these are often the same people who also somehow manage to wangle their way out of doing their share of the unpleasant work and get more than their fair share of the nice things that everyone wants to do? It's enough to make your blood boil.

---

It isn't just the short-term impact on mood that needs to be considered. If you repeatedly see a peer blatantly getting away with doing less, yet still being rewarded the same (or more!), does it motivate you to work harder? Absolutely not – and you may well think: 'If they can get away with it, why should I work myself into the ground?' The whole performance of the team is at risk of heading downhill fast when this type of situation isn't managed properly.

---

We aren't saying it's *easy* to manage the team fairly. In reality, it's a potential minefield of difficult decisions. So let's have a go at tackling a real-life scenario.

---

You are Melanie's manager. Prior to her going on maternity leave, Melanie was contracted to do 35 hours per week spread over five days. Having returned to work, she now works part-time and is contracted to do 14 hours per week spread over two days.

**Issue 1:** Every week you have a one-hour team meeting, which everyone is expected to attend. If Melanie attends the team meeting every week, she will be spending 250%

more of her time in team meetings than everyone else, leaving proportionately less time to do the work in her job description.

---

- Is it fair to Melanie that she attends every weekly team meeting?
- Is it fair to Melanie's team that she attends every weekly team meeting?

*Consider your answers in the context that this is the symptom of a wider problem: Melanie typically needs at least half a day (25% of her working week) just to catch up on emails, do her admin and attend this meeting before she can even start doing any work. This is proportionately more than her peers need.*

---

**Issue 2:** An opportunity (with limited budget) has come up for two people in the team to do a ten-day training course, which will mean that they will be qualified to do some new and prestigious work that the department will be offering to their customers. Like everyone else in the team, Melanie would like to do the qualification. However, to make this investment in her worthwhile, after completing the qualification, she would need to spend her 14 hours doing the new prestigious work, leaving her no time to do her share of the regular work in her job description.

**THINK ABOUT IT**

- Should Melanie be selected to go on the training course? Think about your answer from her point of view and from that of her peers.

*Consider this in the context of the fact that Melanie works in the UK, and under the law of her country she has the right not to be excluded from training opportunities just because she works part-time.*

**Issue 3:** Sam is Melanie's peer and his performance has recently gone downhill. When you ask him why, he says that he's very demotivated because he feels like he's constantly picking up more than his fair share of Melanie's unpleasant tasks. Sam shows you the workflow statistics for the last six months, which undeniably demonstrate that although Melanie was originally scheduled to do her fair share of this work, she has completed less than a quarter of it and Sam has indeed picked up most of the remaining 75%. Sam explains that Melanie always has a plausible reason for not doing what she's assigned to do, for example she had a hospital appointment. But he's also fed up with seeing her spending all morning catching up on emails and going on team lunches when he's carrying her workload.

**THINK ABOUT IT**

- How do you manage Sam?
- How do you manage Melanie?
- Do you need to make any changes to the way that you're managing the team's workload?

*Consider your answers in the context that Melanie has previously said that she feels overwhelmed with the amount of work she has to do in two days, and that she doesn't feel that just because she works part-time she should be expected to work overtime or miss team lunches when everyone else attends.*

From working through the examples above, you may well have seen that making fair management decisions isn't always easy – the law is on your back and you're trying to keep everyone happy when sometimes it just feels impossible to do so. So let's take a look at ways to solve such problems.

## How can you ensure everyone feels like they have been treated justly?

Seeing as we talked about cake at the start of the chapter, let's use cake as an analogy to help us here too. Firstly, imagine that the team's workload is a cake. To keep everyone motivated, you need to slice that cake up fairly and give everyone in the team a fair and reasonable share.

Now imagine there's a second cake, which equates to all of the rewards that can be offered to the team, such as money available for bonuses and development opportunities. To keep people motivated, the slice of the second cake needs to be roughly equal in size to the slice of the first cake that they took.

---

**KEY TERM**

In psychological terms, this is known as **equity theory**, a term first proposed by John Adams in the 1960s. The basic idea of equity theory asserts that people will be happy if they can see that:

1. The amount that they are putting in roughly equals the reward that they get back.
2. Their ratio of input to output is broadly similar to other people doing similar work.

To ensure fairness, it's important that *proportionately* each member's share of the workload is roughly equal, resulting also in a fair distribution of rewards. You should neither exclude any member of the team from rewards they are entitled to, nor over-indulge anyone with more than their fair share.

---

Being practical, it might not always be possible to proportion everyone up exactly. But most people are reasonable and accept a bit of give and take, even if it isn't working in their favour. However, where problems arise is when people can consistently see that someone is taking too small a piece of the 'work' cake and/or receiving too big a piece of the 'reward' cake. When people are disgruntled, this can indicate that your cake has been divided unfairly – or at the very least, they perceive this to be the case.

---

 To be fair to all people in your team and keep them motivated, you should:

- Monitor both how fairly you have divided up the work-load *and* whether the work has actually been done by the person to whom it was allocated.

- Address the situation if a member of the team is regularly generating significantly less work output than other members. See Chapter P: 'Poor Performance' for more guidance.

- Monitor how fairly you have divided up the rewards of the team and ensure that a person's input to the team is reflected in terms of the reward that they receive.

- Find out what rewards motivate specific individuals in your team. Some people may be more motivated by doing varied work projects, others by gaining new qualifications. Wherever possible, try to 'push the buttons' that matter most to your team members.

- Remember that if there aren't enough of certain types of reward to go around, you may need to compensate those who miss out with other rewards so that they don't feel unjustly treated.

---

And finally, remember the lesson my teacher taught: when she cut the cake for the children, they became disgruntled if it wasn't cut up fairly. However, when the children took responsibility for dividing the cake themselves, they were more accepting of the outcome and had a vested interest in ensuring that it really was fair. When appropriate, try to treat people like adults and get them to help you make the decision about what workload and rewards are fair.

---

 Distribute workloads and rewards justly among the team, as otherwise this may cause team members to lose motivation and become dissatisfied.

---

# K: Kindness

*If you step on people in this life, you're going to come back as a cockroach.*

Willie Davis

As much as managers might like it, our personal lives don't magically cease to exist the moment we step through the office door. Employees will regularly face personal circumstances that have an impact during working hours. While it isn't a manager's job to solve these problems, through talking to many employees, a manager's attitude towards them during these difficult times can make or break a working relationship.

This chapter will give you a flavour of some real-life employee issues which have a knock-on impact upon managers. You will be given various different scenarios and you should consider how you would handle each situation. An explanation of what really did happen, and the impact that this had on the employees concerned, will be given after each scenario.

---

**Scenario 1:** You are working abroad helping to organize an international award ceremony, which is your company's major annual event. A couple of days before the ceremony, a member of your team gets a phone call to say that her husband

has been rushed to hospital with suspected meningitis and needs to fly home urgently. **What do you do?**

- Note that a team of twenty other employees are abroad with you preparing to organize the event, some of whom are more junior, some more senior.

*What actually happened*
*The manager concerned told her employee that she could not fly home because it was a business-critical time and she could not be released. Several hours later, a more senior manager heard about this decision and overturned it by organizing a flight so the employee could leave immediately.*

*The employee said that she could never forgive her manager for refusing to allow her to see her husband when there was a possibility he could have died. Ultimately her team coped fine without her, and her husband, although seriously ill, was OK.*

---

**Scenario 2:** A normally calm and happy member of your team is very upset one day because her pet goldfish has died. She is very distracted from her work. **How do you manage the situation?**

*What actually happened*
*The manager concerned felt that her team member's reaction was completely over the top, so she made light of the*

situation and asked her to get on with her work. While this probably doesn't seem at all unreasonable, it's fascinating that in a feedback exercise over two years later, the team member gave very negative comments about how her manager handled this situation and wrote that it had contributed towards disliking the manager ever since – this was just one example of how she regularly treated her staff insensitively.

Even if you think that someone is being ridiculous, if you can see that a normally calm employee is genuinely very upset, it can be beneficial for the longer term to invest in some short-term kindness, such as taking them for a cup of coffee and a chat. You should never force someone to share private information, but it can be helpful to offer a listening ear. It's also worth noting that sometimes, reactions like this can be a sign that there's a deeper personal issue going on, and it gives you an opportunity to build trust and respect with that person. This may help your employees if they feel they need to disclose something more serious to you in future.

---

**CASE STUDY**

**Scenario 3:** Toby works in a large accountancy organization and finds out on his way to work one day that his younger brother has been hit by a car. His brother critically ill in hospital, Toby is absent from work that day to visit his bedside along with his family. Tragically, his brother dies, and

Toby needs time off from work to make arrangements for the funeral and to console his family. He then has to take time off to attend the funeral and take care of his brother's belongings. **Upon Toby's return to work, you need to make a decision: how many days of annual leave will you deduct for his absence?**

Note that:
- Toby has not attended work for fifteen days this year.
- He is entitled to twenty days of annual leave this year, which he hasn't used.
- Company policy allows you to give Toby up to ten days of compassionate leave without HR permission, and more at HR's discretion.

### *What actually happened*
*Toby was asked to take twelve of the fifteen days as annual leave. He was given three days of compassionate leave: one for the day his brother died and two for the funeral. Toby was upset with his manager's decision, feeling that he had the flexibility and good reason to offer him the full ten days' leave, if not more, if HR had been consulted (which they weren't).*

*Despite previously working many hours of overtime, Toby has now decided to do the bare minimum of work for his manager. Toby also feels that his manager has failed to recognize how desperately he needs a proper break to help the grieving process, particularly around Christmas with his family. Both of these things are made more difficult for Toby given that he has only eight days of annual leave left.*

**Scenario 4:** A member of your team breaks down in floods of tears one day during a team meeting. She is beside herself with distress. When you ask her what is wrong, she eventually tells you that for several months she has been coming to terms with news she had been surprised to receive: that her father will be undergoing gender reassignment. **How do you react to her immediate distress?**

### What actually happened

*The manager concerned handled this situation very well. It was obvious that her employee was in no fit state to continue working that day, so she gave her permission to go home for the rest of the day and take the following day (Friday) off so that she would have a few consecutive days of rest. She suggested it might be helpful for the employee to visit her doctor to get some support, and provided the telephone number for the Employee Assistance Programme (who could provide free and confidential counselling). She did not disclose the reason for the person's absence to the team, as it was a highly private matter.*

*This is a good example of a manager acting wisely within their boundaries. Managers cannot be expected to solve this kind of issue, but they can help to support an individual. The employee did peruse the help options sug-gested, and this helped her to cope better, and therefore perform better in her role over the following weeks and months.*

---

**Scenario 5:** A member of your team is trying to sell her house, and a surveyor has been given the keys to do a survey while she's at work. When the surveyor leaves her house at around midday, he closes the door and realizes that he has left both his keys and her keys inside the house. He has rung your team member to say that if she can't get home, he will organize for a locksmith to come and change the locks, as he can't wait all day at her house. **Your team member has offered either to take half a day's holiday to go home, or to go home and come back. What do you tell her?**

Note that:
- She does not have access to the work computer system from home.
- She has some important work to do before tomorrow.
- She lives at least a 1½-hour round-trip drive from work.

### What actually happened
*If the employee had gone home and returned, that would have meant she would have done at least six hours of driv-ing in one day, which her manager felt was unnecessary.*

*He thought that it was quite harsh to make her take half a day's holiday, so he transferred all of the necessary computer information onto a secure USB stick and allowed her to work from home for the rest of the day on her own computer. The employee was very grateful and completed all of her work, saying she actually benefited from having time to do this work in the peace and quiet of her home environment.*

---

Key to successful management is the ability to realize when employees genuinely need you to show them some compassion, and when they are simply trying to take advantage of you. We aren't suggesting that managers should be doormats, but we do advocate that managers show a level of compassion that reflects both the situation at hand and the level of distress a person is experiencing. Look for signs of acute distress and try to empathize with the situation, asking yourself: 'How would I want to be treated in this situation?'

---

**IF YOU REMEMBER ONE THING** Employees will bring their problems into the office. Where a manager shows compassion and empathizes with a member of staff experiencing a personal problem, they will develop a stronger relationship with that person.

---

# L: Life–work balance

*The time to relax is when you don't have time for it.*
Sydney J. Harris

Paul worked in a finance organization renowned for having a culture where long hours were the norm. And for Paul the specific nature of his job meant the pressure on his life–work balance was even more exaggerated, as he worked on company takeover deals. When a deal was imminent, there was a lot of pressure to act quickly and close the deal, so there was no time to take it easy.

Paul had been working on an important deal for his manager, and had so much to do that he worked constantly in the office for over 48 hours. That's more than two solid days and nights in a row.

Total exhaustion kicked in and Paul, who was in his late thirties, suffered a heart attack, which he thankfully survived.

After Paul had been taken to hospital, HR tried to investigate why Paul had become so unwell. When they uncovered the pattern of his working hours, they questioned his line manager about why he had done this. His manager simply replied: 'Well, there was work to do, so why wouldn't he be working continuously?'

What is the difference between stress and pressure?

It's critical that managers understand the difference between stress and pressure. Pressure can be energizing; it can push people to try harder and perform at their best.

Stress should never be viewed as something that has a positive impact upon a person. Stress is an adverse condition where a person is placed under excessive pressure, or where they have other unreasonable demands placed upon them.

And stress has the effect of damaging people's health. While under stress, your body produces the hormone cortisol to keep your blood pressure high and your blood sugar levels up. This is our primitive 'fight or flight' response, and in evolutionary terms it was useful to help us prepare for battles or run away from our enemies. Cortisol levels then fall once the stressor has gone away.

However, in our high-stress culture, the cortisol levels in our body remain high for prolonged periods, which can have very serious effects on our health – there's a reason why cortisol is nicknamed 'the death hormone'. And let's throw a bit of premature ageing in just for fun. Have you ever noticed how prime ministers and presidents age dramatically after they step up to their demanding new job?

**REMEMBER THIS!!!**

Just as managers cannot ask someone to touch a dangerous plug at work, they also have a duty of care not to damage someone's health due to stress. Managers must monitor when pressure has turned into stress and intervene to prevent harm to a person's health.

You'll find some more advice on stress management in Chapter N: 'Not Coping'. However, this chapter focuses on how a manager can help employees to reduce stress through achieving a sensible life–work balance.

A key way to do this is to ensure that people experience adequate rest from work. There are different types of breaks, and it's important that your staff get all four:

- 'Holiday rest' – this is where a person has a number of days away from work, and it's part of their annual leave entitlement detailed within their employment contract.

- 'Weekly rest' – whole days when you don't come into work, ensuring that you take a break of at least 24 consecutive hours every week or 48 hours every two weeks.

- 'Daily rest' – the break between finishing one day's work and starting the next, with at least eleven hours' break between ending work and starting the next day.

- 'Rest breaks' – e.g. tea or lunch, ensuring that a person has at least a twenty-minute break in the middle of their working day. If someone is working at a computer, it's helpful to encourage them to take a short break away from the screen each hour, for example, to alleviate eye-strain.

These figures are given as guidelines, so check the legal situation for your own country and industry. Some organizations ask their employees to sign away their legal entitlement to breaks, but remember that guidelines like these are in place for a reason.

**THINK ABOUT IT**

- How often do you manage to get the amount of rest as outlined in the guidelines above?
- How does your manager's behaviour contribute to your answer?

**CASE STUDY**

Here's a real-life example of how long hours can affect performance. Kelly works in the advertising industry, her year's work culminating in a large annual awards ceremony. In the month building up to the ceremony, Kelly's manager would regularly (say, five nights out of seven) ring her at around 2.00am or 3.00am, to ask her questions such as: 'Did you remember to put that slide into the presentation?' Because of these continual interruptions, Kelly found that she was becoming exhausted and that her performance during the workday went down at this critical time because she was too tired to function. This was the same manager who would regularly, throughout the year, summon Kelly to explain where she was going when she packed up her things to leave at 10.30pm, having been at work for fourteen hours straight.

---

It isn't only your performance that can suffer alongside your life–work balance. Research has shown that:

- Employees' satisfaction with their life–work balance was one of two strongest predictors of customer satisfaction. The other factor was employees' general satisfaction with their jobs. (Sue Shellenbarger, 'Surveys Link Satisfaction of Employees, Customers', *Wall Street Journal*, 1999)

- In a survey by the Corporate Leadership Council of over 50,000 individuals in 2008, life–work balance was among the top three most important things that attract a potential employee to a new company.

- The Corporate Leadership Council also found that only 16% of employees are satisfied with the life–work practices offered by their organization, and nearly a third of employees are reducing their effort levels to better meet personal commitments.

Kelly's manager rang her repeatedly in the early hours of the morning. Is contacting someone in the middle of the night ever acceptable?

The answer to the above question is 'yes' – *if* it's an essential part of your job, for example because you are a doctor on call. This would normally be agreed up-front as part of the negotiation of being offered and accepting your job (i.e. it's part of your 'psychological contract').

Problems with life–work balance occur when:

- Things happen that you *didn't* sign up for (i.e. breaching the psychological contract). Kelly did not sign up for being called during the night to check if PowerPoint slides were in a presentation. If she had been told this at interview, she would have been very unlikely to take the job.

- Things happen that you *did* sign up for, but that are managed in a way that is unacceptable. For example, as a lawyer, Tony knew that he would occasionally have to work through the night to close a major deal. However, he did not expect that, having worked all day and all night, when he went to pick up his coat at 10.00 the next morning to go home and sleep, he would be told: 'Where are you going? It isn't 5.30pm yet.'

## How to maximize life–work balance during busy periods

Phil is managing a major training operation at a business-critical time. Over the next six months, he's about to have large numbers of trainees through the door, with classes occurring seven days a week from morning until night. But he's managing the situation really well, by:

- Telling people up front at interview what the reality of the situation will be and giving the opportunity to opt out before they sign up for the role.

- Doing his very best to accommodate people's personal requests (e.g. working the roster around important personal commitments, such as attending a friend's wedding).

- Encouraging people to plan their holidays and making sure that they take that break.

- Not rostering people on a late shift and then again on the early shift.

- Ensuring that the workload is divided up fairly so that no one is constantly having to do the late shift that no one wants to do.

- Contingency planning, so if someone is off sick, for example, he doesn't have to call on already exhausted people to fill the gaps.

- Giving everyone lots of notice of when their unsociable hours will be, so that they can make arrangements around that in advance (e.g. childcare arrangements).

- Putting on transport to make getting home after the late shift quicker and easier.

Phil's is a great example of a finding from the Corporate Leadership Council's research on life–work balance: that workload management tactics, not traditional life–work benefits, are the most powerful elements of an effective life–work proposition. They found that organizations that effectively manage their life–work proposition can improve employee discretionary effort levels by 21% and increase employee intent to stay by 33%.

So the next time you start cracking the whip to make your employees stay later and work harder, remember that this could have the opposite effect on them.

---

**IF YOU REMEMBER ONE THING** Managers need to monitor and support the life–work balance of their staff – if it tips too much into a work–work relationship the employee, the manager, and ultimately the organization will suffer.

---

# M: Managing change

*Change is hard because people overestimate the value of what they have and underestimate the value of what they may gain by giving that up.*

James Belasco and Ralph Stayer

---

**Round 1**: Imagine this: you are on a management training course and you've been asked to stand back-to-back with a partner and change three things about your appearance, so that your partner can then guess what you've changed. What three things would you do to change your current appearance?

**Round 2**: After your partner has guessed, you then have to change *another* three things. What would you do next?

**Round 3**: And before you start to groan too much (everyone else on the training course would be by now), we are going to ask you to change yet *another* three things.

---

When we experienced this exercise on a training course, having changed a total of nine things, we were then asked to stop (thank goodness, we'd all have been in our underwear soon otherwise) and identify what the group had done to 'change'. We identified things such as: watches had been taken off, buttons undone, belts turned round, trousers rolled up, earrings removed, hair untied, etc. Did you think of the same kind of things? What do you notice about the way that people think about the word 'change'?

This exercise demonstrated that people subconsciously interpret the word change as 'taking away' or 'keeping something but making it different'. We typically don't enjoy these interpretations of change much; it's insightful to watch people trying to sneak their watches back on between rounds, aiming to revert to the comfortable and familiar way that they were before.

Very few people had *added* items in order to change, and those who had, had typically displayed this behaviour only during round 3 when they were getting desperate.

**Round 4**: The final stage of the exercise was to change three more things about our appearance, but this time we were specifically told to change our appearance by *adding* new items. Someone grabbed a piece of flipchart paper and made a beautiful skirt; the board-wiper cloth became a napkin; pens went behind ears and we borrowed each other's scarves, coats and glasses. We all looked truly lovely! It was fascinating to observe the energy levels increase in the room. When we viewed change as an opportunity to be innovative and gain new things, it became much more fun and enjoyable.

As a manager, it's useful to understand that when a change is announced, people's first stop on the change journey is likely to be, 'What will I lose as a result of this change?' rather than, 'What will I gain as a result of this change?' That's why people so often resist change at first. It can also explain why people are so resistant to something as seemingly insignificant as moving desks – they like sitting next to the window, being near the coffee machine or in close proximity to people they get on with, and they fear losing this. They forget to evaluate the things they will gain as a result of the change. It's usually only over time that they come to realize the benefits that the change has brought, and become more accepting of it.

## Why are we programmed to be so resistant to change?

To answer this question it's useful to explore the neuroscience of how our brain deals with change.

---

Our brains have two key areas when it comes to memory. The first is called the pre-frontal cortex, at the front of your brain just above your eyebrows, and it controls **working memory**. Working memory is involved when we need to think consciously – for example, the first time we get behind the wheel of a car and learn how to drive. Our working memory is very limited in capacity and is energy-intensive, which is why learners can feel overwhelmed during their lesson and exhausted after it. Having too many things to think about at once drains our working memory.

The second key area, the basal ganglia, right in the centre of our brain, processes our routine, habitual activities, our **subconscious memory**. This area is involved when you've been driving for years and you can do it without really thinking about it. This type of memory is far less energy-intensive because it works on well-established neural pathways, shaped through extensive practice.

---

**THINK ABOUT IT**

Imagine that the capacity of working memory is equivalent to one cubic foot. How big do you think the capacity of your subconscious memory would be? According to Dr David Rock, an expert in neuroscience, in this analogy our subconscious memory would be equivalent in size to the entire Milky Way!

---

So given the vast difference in capacity between working and subconscious memory, you can see why our brain is programmed to run as much activity as possible on auto-pilot, in order to free up working memory for the things that really need it. In a fantastic article called 'Neuroscience of Leadership', David Rock and Jeffrey Schwartz argue that this is why we find change painful. Our brains are wired to have a clear preference for habitual behaviour and activities, and when managers want us to change quickly they are literally battling with evolution.

## How can managers support their teams to find change less painful?

As we have seen, we are predisposed to find change difficult. Here are five tips for managers to help them to make change events less painful.

1. **Help people to see the positives.** When people are evaluating whether to accept or resist a change, they will typically evaluate, 'What will I lose vs. what will I gain?' If they stand to gain more than they lose, they will accept the change and put effort in to make it work. If they stand to lose more than they gain, then they will resist it. But remember that people will be more likely to see the negatives than the positives, so as a manager, you should try to (sensitively) point out the positives of what people will gain from the situation.

2. **Get people involved in solving problems.** When there are difficult problems to solve, it can really help to put the issue 'on the table' and ask people how they think it should be solved. For example, this has been used successfully by organizations that, due to recession, have no choice but to cut staff costs. The advantage of employee involvement is that people have the opportunity to find ways to protect the things that matter the most to them (their 'must haves'), and in order to protect these they may be prepared to offer a concession in return. They therefore propose the concessions

rather than having them forced upon them. This shows the critical difference between being forced to comply with a change that has been imposed vs. committing to a strategy that you have helped to develop.

3. **Support people through the 'change curve'.** The 'change curve' theory, developed by Elisabeth Kubler-Ross, asserts that people follow a fixed series of responses to change, namely shock, denial, anger, depression and finally acceptance. It's normal for people to have these responses to change. A good manager will recognize that people need time to get through each stage and critically will aim to support people to move to the next stage as quickly as possible. This requires managers to be able to identify what stage individuals are at and offer support appropriate to that stage. As an example, after mass redundancies, managers can speed up acceptance of the situation for the 'survivors' if they work hard to make their remaining team members feel valued and that the organization is committed to them.

4. **Be fair.** People can experience additional pain to that arising from the change itself, when they feel that, to add insult to injury, the change was unfairly handled. It's critical at times of change that decision-making is transparent and that managers can justify the decisions they have made.

5.  **Give people timely information.** Managers can make a bad situation worse when they fail to update people as to how a change is progressing. For example, Jennifer was told by her manager that redundancies would be occurring in her immediate team and that he would let her know within approximately two to three weeks whether she would be at risk of losing her job. With a mortgage to pay, Jennifer panicked for weeks, although she eventually realized that a couple of other people had been made redundant. Her manager never got back to her. For some people, not knowing what is happening is the worst part – and once they know one way or the other they can move forward. If you have promised people an update but can't give them an answer, at the very least, update them that you don't have the answer yet and that you will get back to them again at 'x' time. And then get back to them!

## How can managers encourage change to be sustained?

Finally, remember in our change exercise how people tried to sneak their watches back on and 'change back'? This is also an example of slipping back into old habits. Linking back to the neuroscience previously discussed, even though we can engage conscious thought to do things differently, the brain is pre-programmed to want to get you back on autopilot as soon as possible. This is one of the reasons why it's so difficult to change habits in the long term. We've got new neural pathways to build and quite frankly it would be much easier to use the old ones.

**If you want change to be sustained, it's vital to:**

1. Keep reminding people of the changes that they need to make, to jog their memory.

2. Recognize and reward when you see someone displaying changed behaviour, to motivate them to keep the new behaviour conscious, and to reinforce the thinking that it's worth that extra effort it takes to change.

---

 As change can often be viewed as a negative thing, a manager should focus on the positives and what will be gained from change. If you want to see the new behaviour become the norm, remember to **remind** and **reward**.

---

# N: Not coping

*There cannot be a stressful crisis next week.*
*My schedule is already full.*

Henry Kissinger

In Chapter L: 'Life–work balance', we explored how failing to give people adequate time away from work can cause them to suffer from stress. Given that stress management is such an important part of a manager's job, this chapter explores work-related stress in more detail.

The British government's Health and Safety Executive (HSE) has done some excellent research into what causes people to suffer from work-related stress. They conclude that there are six key causes:

1. **Demands:** Where the work that is expected from a person exceeds their ability to cope, due to the amount of work, the setting in which they are working, or their personal capability.
   *E.g. Paul from Chapter L: 'Life–work balance', who had so much work to do that he was in the office for more than 48 consecutive hours and then suffered a heart attack.*

2. **Relationships:** When an individual is subjected to unacceptable behaviour from other employees.
   *E.g. Alice's manager did not speak a single word to her for over three months after Alice had resigned from her job (despite sitting within a few metres of her).*

3. **Control:** Where an individual does not have enough say about how and when they do their work and take their breaks.

   *E.g. Kelly from Chapter L: 'Life–work balance', who could not prevent her manager from ringing her in the middle of the night to ask her questions.*

4. **Role:** Where an individual does not understand their role, responsibilities or purpose.

   *E.g. Gary from Chapter I: 'Induction', who repeatedly tried to ask his manager what he was meant to be doing, to which his manager simply replied, 'Work it out yourself.'*

5. **Support**: Where an individual does not have sufficient access to the information, resources, encouragement or advice needed to do their job.

   *E.g. A member of Claire's team was under-performing to the point where it was having a clearly detrimental impact on the rest of the team. However, Claire had never been taught how to formally 'performance manage' someone, and her manager simply told her to avoid 'going there' without offering an alternative solution.*

6. **Change:** When a change (big or small) is not managed or communicated well.

   *E.g. Jennifer from Chapter M: 'Managing change' was told that she was at risk of losing her job and that she would be told either way within a couple of weeks. Two years later, she still hadn't been told the answer. She assumed she was safe by then, but the initial few weeks of uncertainty had been unnecessarily stressful.*

---

 Think of examples of when you or your team members have suffered from stress caused by each of these areas.

---

## The bucket metaphor

You can think of a person's ability to cope like a bucket:

- The capacity inside the bucket represents how much pressure the person can take before they experience a negative stress reaction. The size of people's buckets will vary. Some people will have large buckets because they are naturally calm and able to take life in their stride. Other people will have smaller buckets.

- The water inside the bucket represents the level of pressure a person is under. There can be a single source of pressure or many different sources. Once the bucket is full, it takes only a single drop to make it overflow and cause a stress reaction, hence the reason why something seemingly insignificant can cause a meltdown.

The bucket analogy explains why it's important that managers monitor the impact of both large incidents and, crucially, the cumulative effect of smaller ones. Managers also need to remember that a team member's metaphorical bucket may already be filled with stress caused by their personal life, which may mean that their capacity to tolerate work-related stress is reduced.

## Assessing whether your staff are at risk from work-related stress

The following questionnaire gives a sample of questions from the HSE Indicator Tool, which managers can use to evaluate the levels of stress that their team members are under. A full copy of the questionnaire, instructions on how to use it and a tool to help you analyse the results are available at: www.management-handbook.com

- The questionnaire can be completed anonymously, depending on your relationship with your team.

- You will need to agree with them before completing the questionnaire whether the data will be anonymous, how the results will be used, who the data will be shared with, and why the questionnaire is being done.

- It's recommended that completion of the questionnaire is optional, emphasizing the benefits to individuals of them participating in the exercise – you are trying to help to monitor their stress levels, so that you can take action against problem areas.

**Rate how much you agree with the following questions:**

1 = strongly agree (potentially leading to high stress)
5 = strongly disagree (low stress)

| Section A: Demands | |
|---|---|
| Different groups at work demand things from me that are hard to combine | |
| I have unachievable deadlines | |
| I am unable to take sufficient breaks | |
| I am pressured to work long hours | |

| Section B: Relationships | |
|---|---|
| I am subject to personal harassment in the form of unkind words or behaviour | |
| There is friction or anger between colleagues | |
| I am subject to bullying at work | |
| Relationships at work are strained | |

**Now use this rating scale for the remaining questions:**

1 = strongly disagree (potentially leading to high stress)
5 = strongly agree (low stress)

| Section C: Control | |
|---|---|
| I can decide when to take a break | |
| I have a choice in deciding how I do my work | |
| I have a choice in deciding what I do at work | |
| My working time can be flexible | |

| Section D: Role | |
|---|---|
| I am clear what is expected of me at work | |
| I am clear what my duties and responsibilities are | |
| I am clear about the goals and objectives for my department | |
| I understand how my work fits into the overall aim of the organization | |

| Section E: Support | |
|---|---|
| I can rely on my line manager to help me out with a work problem | |
| I am supported through emotionally demanding work | |
| My line manager encourages me at work | |
| I get help and support I need from colleagues | |

| Section F: Change | |
|---|---|
| I have sufficient opportunities to question managers about change at work | |
| Staff are always consulted about change at work | |
| When changes are made at work, I am clear how they will work out in practice | |

## Interpreting the results and taking action

You can review the data by looking at individual people's questionnaires or by averaging the results of a whole group. You are looking for scores to be high (i.e. more than 4).

For some questions you will be looking for a very

positive result. For example, you would be looking for every single member of your team to strongly disagree (i.e. score 5) with the statement 'I am subject to bullying at work'.

For other questions you may need to be realistic about how positively they can be scored. For example, due to the nature of their work, it may be impossible for every team member to score 5/5 to the question, 'My working time can be flexible'. If scores to this question are low, you should consider what you can do (within the boundaries of what is possible) to give as much flexibility as you are able.

The HSE recommends that you select specific areas for improvement, take appropriate action and repeat the questionnaire process regularly (i.e. every six months). It's critical that you are seen to take action on the results so that it's not simply seen as a paper exercise.

---

**THINK ABOUT IT** What could you do to reduce work-related stress levels for each of the six areas (Demands, Relationships, Control, Role, Support, Change)? Some tips for doing this can be found at www.management-handbook.com, along with the full version of the indicator tool.

---

**IF YOU REMEMBER ONE THING** Everybody has a limit to the amount of stress that they can take on – a manager should try to monitor these levels among their staff and where they are high or rising, find ways to reduce them.

---

# O: Operational problems

*We have no simple problems or easy decisions
after kindergarten.*

John W. Turk

Wouldn't it be fantastic for managers if they didn't have any issues coming from team members or customers? Managerial life would be so easy! Unfortunately this isn't the case and things don't always run smoothly. So, a key role of a manager is to be able to successfully deal with problems that disrupt our day-to-day operations.

Managers constantly have to make decisions:

- Severe snow is forecast – should I send the team home early today?
- 50% of the team are off ill – what do we do to cover the workload?
- Should I give compassionate leave for someone to attend a friend's funeral, or should they take it as annual leave?
- The team has a constant backlog of work – should we recruit an extra member to the team?
- A member of the team has not done what I needed him to do, despite asking him repeatedly – what should I do?

This chapter will support you in resolving issues like these.

## Understanding your boundaries of responsibility

The first step to problem-solving is to assess whether a problem is within your boundaries of responsibility. Think about your job as a circle with a big white line around it. That white line represents the boundary of your responsibility. You should make decisions on everything within your circle and should refer things that fall outside it.

Successful managers are very clear about what lies within their boundary of responsibility and what doesn't – and act accordingly.

So how do we know what is within our boundary of responsibility? Clearly the exact definition of what falls inside your 'white line' will vary from manager to manager and across organizations. However, here are three things that can really help:

1. **Being very familiar with organizational policies.** For example, a bereavement policy may state that unpaid leave can be given at a manager's discretion, in which case you know that this decision falls within your boundary of responsibility. Read all of the applicable policies and keep yourself abreast of updates.

2. **Keep your manager informed.** Keep your manager updated about decisions that you have made in a timely manner. That way, if you made the wrong decision, or

the decision wasn't yours to make, this will help you to better understand your boundary. It also gives you an opportunity to rectify any bad decisions.

3. **Risk-assess.** When making decisions that you think do fall just inside your boundary, ask yourself, 'If I make a poor decision, am I likely to face any financial, legal, reputational or personnel issues as a result?' If the answer is 'yes', it may be better to escalate the issue just in case and use this opportunity to clarify whether it was your decision to make or not.

---

 There's a fine line between not escalating issues enough and constantly bombarding other people, such as your own manager, with them. It might be worth asking your manager whether you are getting the balance right between 'acting' and 'escalating' and whether you are overstepping or understepping the mark when it comes to managing your boundaries of responsibility.

---

## Managing upwards

Sometimes you know what action needs to be taken to resolve a problem, but you also know that it isn't your decision to make. In this situation, it can be useful to consider how you can influence more senior management to get other people to come around to your point of view.

Most of us will have a natural way of trying to influence others. Four common ways of influencing include:

- **Asserting:** Clearly stating your point of view and what you want to happen next.

- **Data-driven:** A rational approach, trying to persuade the listener to accept your point of view through the use of facts and figures.

- **Inspiring:** Using a high-energy style, you seek to motivate the listener to take the desired action, through exciting and enthusing them about the rewards that lie ahead.

- **Consulting:** Asking others to come up with possible solutions, with the rationale that people are more bought-in to solutions that they shape. Ideally, they will come up with the solution you have already thought of. However, you should be prepared to take their feedback on board and change your mind when using this style.

---

- We've just introduced four different influencing styles. Try to think of people you know who each clearly use one of the styles.
- Which style do you think you use most/ least often?

---

# When to use each influencing style

Although most of us have a natural influencing style, we don't have to use it all the time. If you want more gravitas to influence a situation, think about the best style to get the outcome you want. The following table will give you a guide as to when an influencing style can be useful and when you need to be careful using it.

| STYLE | USEFUL WHEN ... | BE CAREFUL WHEN ... |
|---|---|---|
| **Asserting** | You have needs, standards and expectations that are very important to you. | There are other people with strong differing opinions, as you could get into conflict. |
| **Data-driven** | You have robust information that really supports your case. | You are talking about very emotional issues and you could come across as very insensitive. |
| **Inspiring** | Both parties have common values and goals, which can be achieved through your strategy. | You are working with cynical people who don't fully trust you, as this could make them even more cynical. |
| **Consulting** | You need the other party to be really committed to the solution. The other party is emotionally involved. | You have definitely decided on a course of action and consultation is therefore a pointless exercise. |

TRY IT NOW!

Think about a problem that you are currently struggling to solve.

- What influencing style have you been using to resolve that issue?
- What influencing style might help you most to resolve it?

## Managing downwards

Even when something is within your boundary of responsibility and you know what action needs to be taken to solve the issue, when others are involved, getting them to *take* action is another issue altogether. We love the title of a book written by Warren Bennis, *Managing People is Like Herding Cats*.

Influencing styles can be really helpful when managing downwards and trying to solve issues.

CASE STUDY

Vicky was struggling because a couple of members of her team simply would not do the work that they had been asked to do, even though they were perfectly capable of doing it. Vicky had tried her very best to motivate and inspire them to take action, but it simply wasn't working.

At her wits' end, Vicky deliberately changed the way that she communicated with the under-performers in her team. Rather than constantly trying to **inspire** them, which was her typical way of doing things, she became **assertive** and clearly informed the individuals what needed to be done and by when. This change of influencing style had the desired result and the work was completed.

---

Vicky demonstrates how useful it can be to **change your own behaviour** in order to influence others to think or act in the way you would like them to. This is a very useful tool if you feel like you're hitting a brick wall when trying to solve a problem.

## Employee involvement

The **consulting** influencing style picks up on a very useful psychological technique when it comes to solving difficult problems – involving the affected people in the decision-making process. If you empower those affected to come up with the solution, they can often come up with the most fair and creative way forward. You can see the difference between:

A. Imposing times to cover difficult shifts on people, without consultation; and

B. Explaining what the problem is and asking those affected to come up with possible solutions that are palatable.

Sometimes managers can feel that it's their sole responsibility to make difficult decisions – that's what they are there to do. However, good managers realize that employee involvement is a genuinely great strategy to use, particularly in the face of difficult or sensitive problems. As indicated in the influencing styles table above, when consulting with people for their solutions to problems, just make sure that you are genuinely open to the suggestions that your employees make, and that the answer isn't a foregone conclusion.

---

**IF YOU REMEMBER ONE THING** Overcome day-to-day problems by identifying your boundary of responsibilities, and use influencing styles where appropriate to arrive at the solution. Take inspiration from these words: 'Power is the ability to influence the decisions of others.' (Roger Fisher)

---

# P: Poor performance

*Treat people the way they are and they will stay that way.*
*Treat people the way they can become and*
*they will become that way.*

Johann Wolfgang von Goethe

Poor performance is an important problem because it can hold teams back, be very emotional for anybody affected, and can lead to a formal disciplinary process with HR involved. So let's take a look at a real-life case of poor performance from the employee's point of view and then from the manager's.

---

### The employee's perspective

59-year-old Jean had worked for a company for over fifteen years. She was highly diligent, always working her contracted hours and trying her very best. She was, perhaps, almost too diligent, her keen eye for detail often slowing her down in her quest for perfection.

Jean would be the first to admit that she struggled to meet deadlines, although her performance had always been rated as satisfactory in her annual performance review. Her manager, Mary, had only once informally mentioned to Jean that she needed to try harder to meet her deadlines.

During Jean's most recent appraisal she was told by her manager that she had been classified in the bottom 10% of performers, meaning she would be put on a performance improvement plan. Jean's understanding was that this was an informal process designed to support her, so she could cope with her workload better. In theory this sounded sensible – she could do with some support to manage her heavy workload. However, when Jean questioned the implications of being classified in the bottom 10%, her manager simply said: 'To be honest, it's up or out.' This came as a shock to Jean, who had no idea that her performance had been so unacceptable.

Far from helping her to improve, Jean felt the management team were crushing every last bit of confidence that she had left. She was forced to attend a weekly meeting, where her manager would scrutinize and criticize her against targets, and the whole process felt like an interrogation. The only training that she was offered to help her improve was an emotional intelligence course. Jean felt that this had no relevance whatsoever to helping her meet deadlines. Despite the pressure she was under, Jean tried her very hardest. She worked throughout her holiday and at evenings and weekends to try to catch up. It was beginning to make her ill, but she felt scared to say anything to her manager, as it could be a black mark against her performance.

One month into her performance improvement plan she was told that she was on track. Then, a new, less experienced manager who had never met Jean in person before, and was based in a different country, took over her monitoring and Jean was told that actually, she still wasn't performing satisfactorily.

At this point, Jean's health began to deteriorate and she sought medical help in the form of sleeping tablets and anti-anxiety medication. Jean's doctors prescribed her valium to enable her to get through her weekly performance improvement meetings. Her managers recognized that she was struggling, but offered her no support or other job options. She either had to improve or she would face the employment termination process.

After three months Jean was told that she had demonstrated that she *had* improved against the measures originally set. However, her management team had decided that she *now* needed to improve in other new areas, and told her that she had one final month to improve before she would face formal disciplinary action. At this point, Jean asked her doctor to refer her for counselling to help her cope with the stress she was under. She was referred to a psychiatrist who immediately signed Jean off sick with work-related stress.

After six months of sick leave, Jean wanted to try to return to work and rectify the situation. However, far from being sympathetic that they had made Jean so unwell, her management simply told her that after an easing-in period of two weeks of part-time work, she would be straight back on the performance improvement plan, and would face formal disciplinary procedures for poor performance at the end of a month.

A desperate and broken Jean eventually sought the advice of a lawyer and ultimately was paid almost a year's salary in return for a mutual agreement to end her employment contract. Jean ended her career feeling like a failure and over a year after she left the organization she still comments how much the situation damaged her and continues to cause her distress.

---

### The manager's perspective

Jean's organization had a policy whereby managers were required to classify a certain percentage of employees as poor performers.

Unfortunately for Jean, despite her obvious efforts and sound work ethic, compared to others in the team, she was performing poorly. Although everyone was clearly under pressure, while Jean was struggling to work on four projects at a time, others in the team were able to work on seven projects at a time. During the year, Jean's manager Mary had tried to have a quiet word with her to let her know that she needed to meet her deadlines, but the situation hadn't really improved.

Mary had a job to do, which required managing the workflow of the team and overseeing work to ensure that deadlines were met. Mary was under increasing pressure from her own manager to stop Jean from missing her deadlines, and action needed to be taken.

From Mary's point of view, she was following the procedure that she was meant to follow. She was holding (time-consuming) weekly performance improvement meetings with Jean, setting her what she felt were manageable targets. She was aware that Jean was very anxious and upset by the process, which was why she suggested an emotional intelligence course to help Jean communicate better. Given that the performance improvement plan was the first step of the formal disciplinary procedure for poor performance, Mary was aware that the process needed to be taken seriously, with all meetings formally documented.

Although Mary felt that Jean was improving, due to an organizational restructure, a new manager then became responsible for monitoring Jean's performance and the situation was taken out of Mary's hands.

The management team had a discussion about moving Jean into a particular role that would play to her strengths. However, due to factors outside of their control, they decided that this would not be a suitable option at that time. After Jean's sick leave they felt that it was inappropriate to abandon the performance improvement plan, since she was yet to demonstrate that her performance had adequately improved. Simply letting her off the plan would make a mockery of the performance management process and would set a precedent that if you want to get out of being a poor performer, you just go off sick.

**THINK ABOUT IT**

Imagine that you are Jean's manager. How could you have handled the situation better to bring out the best in Jean:

- In the months running up to her annual review?
- During her performance review?
- When working out how to improve Jean's performance?

## Ways to handle the situation

There are a number of ways a manager can handle the situation of a poorly performing team member, including:

- **Giving regular feedback:** Employees need regular, informal feedback about their performance, and support throughout the year. When someone's performance is slipping, try to address this at an early stage and give them continued feedback on their progress.

- **Choosing your words carefully:** Consider your language when giving people difficult messages. If your aim is genuinely to encourage someone to improve, then choose words that build a person's confidence, rather than destroying it.

- **Agreeing stretching yet achievable targets:** Targets help a person understand what is expected of them and give them specific things to aim for. Research has shown that setting specific and challenging goals helps people to achieve more. Where appropriate, encourage the employee to set his/her own stretching targets, which will increase their buy-in. Emphasize the benefits of target-setting and avoid making the person feel as if they are being scrutinized or criticized.

- **Giving the right support:** When giving people training and development to support them to improve their skills, make sure that you are giving them opportunities that will directly solve the problem at hand. Also do not assume that sending someone on a one-day training course will fix the issue at hand. Take time to analyse the root cause of the problem and find effective solutions. In Chapter T: 'Training' you will see how Jean's poor performance issue could have been handled much more effectively with better support.

## Getting to the root cause of the poor performance

When trying to identify what is causing under-performance, it can be useful to try to separate out whether it's caused by low capability (or skill), low motivation (or will) or both of these, as in the 'will–skill' matrix covered in Chapter E: 'Empowerment'.

### High will, Low skill

When someone has a positive attitude to work and is trying hard, it's important to nurture that motivation and encourage that person to improve their skill levels.

You may find it useful to employ a popular coaching framework called 'GROW', developed from the work of Alan Fine, Graham Alexander and Sir John Whitmore. This will help you to structure a discussion identifying what skills the person could benefit from improving. GROW involves finding answers to four key questions:

**G** (Goal) What would improved performance look like?

**R** (Reality) What does current performance look like? What are the current skill gaps?

**O** (Options) What are the options to improve the skills gaps? What would help the person?

**W** (Way forward) Identify a way forward, and create an action plan based on the most suitable options.

The individual is likely to have an idea of why they are struggling and so, wherever possible, try to get them to self-identify what needs to be improved.

## Low will, High skill

You can also use GROW to help to determine the root cause of poor performance when people have the ability to do the job, but seem unmotivated and therefore aren't putting in the effort required.

**G** (Goal) What is the level of commitment expected to complete the current role?

**R** (Reality)  What is the person's current attitude towards work, and what factors are influencing this?
**O** (Options)  What would help the person to feel more motivated and commit to the effort required?
**W** (Way forward)  Identify and action-plan a way forward, based on the most suitable options.

This situation requires trying to get to the bottom of what is causing their lack of motivation. One possible explanation is that they have become complacent and think that they can get away with a slackened attitude to work, perhaps taking long lunch breaks or surfing the internet during working hours. In this instance, the manager needs to make the person aware that this has been observed and is not acceptable.

When a person is not doing the required hours, for example through significant sickness absence or through coming in late or leaving early, it's important to explore whether this is the result of complacency or whether personal issues are impacting their work schedule. It may be appropriate to treat a person with significant personal demands differently to someone who is merely being lazy.

In addition to complacency and personal problems, a lack of 'will' may also be caused by factors to do with their work environment, for example, dissatisfaction with:

- Their relationships with you or other team members – see Chapter Q: 'Quarrels'

- Their reward and recognition – see Chapter W: 'Well done'
- Their personal development – see Chapter T: 'Training'
- Their career progression – see Chapter U: 'Upward progression'

Identifying the root cause of low motivation is very important to finding an appropriate solution. In some cases the individual may identify that they feel like a 'square peg in a round hole' and that the job simply isn't suited to them, in which case it may be helpful to receive career coaching to determine if there's a more suitable career path for them.

**Low will, Low skill**

In this situation you will need to explore both the lack of skill and the low commitment attitude. You might find it helpful to start by exploring a person's 'will', since it may be difficult to help their performance improve if they are not motivated to do so.

## If things still don't improve

You will need to seek further guidance from your manager and HR on how to handle the situation within your company guidelines. However, do your very best to avoid this happening and aim to support your team member to thrive.

**THINK ABOUT IT** Their success is your success. It isn't only your employees' capability or motivation that influences their ability to improve. Their performance improvement (or lack of) is also a direct reflection of your capability as a manager. A manager's attitude and behaviour can bring out both the best and the worst in a person, so always take time out to consider how you interact with your employees and how you leave them feeling.

**IF YOU REMEMBER ONE THING** Where a member of staff is poorly performing, ensure that they are aware of this and offer them ways to improve, having evaluated their 'will' and 'skill' levels.

# Q: Quarrels

*Conflict can destroy a team which hasn't spent time learning
to deal with it.*

Thomas Isgar

Have you ever experienced the feeling of being irritated by
a friend when you've spent too much time with them? They
can really start to get on your nerves. And that's someone
you have *chosen* to be with.

So let's consider work – a place where you may well
spend more of your waking time than anywhere else, asso-
ciating with people you wouldn't normally choose to be
with and may not particularly like! It's a recipe for disaster.

And conflict does happen, and frequently. A report produced by CPP Inc. in 2008 concluded that 85% of employees at all levels experience conflict. Conflicts have a big
knock-on impact on managers. For example, Carol Watson
and Richard Hoffman (1996) concluded that 30–42% of a
manager's time is spent trying to reach agreements with
others when conflicts occur.

This chapter will therefore help you to spot and deal
with workplace conflict. The concepts in this chapter can
be applied both to resolving conflict between individuals
in your team, and conflicts between you and other members of the team. So take a deep breath, count to ten and
read on.

## Signs of conflict

Conflict may be very visible, such as a heated exchange of words or someone breaking down in tears. It may, however, be less obvious. For example, you might become aware that someone is deliberately avoiding you. This can be a particularly difficult situation, because your 'gut feeling' tells you that there's a problem, but you don't know for sure whether there's a conflict going on. Where this is the case, it's worth looking for some of the secondary consequences of conflict, which include:

- Increased amounts of sick leave
- Low morale
- A visible change in behaviour
- Exclusion from social events
- Lots of people resigning one after another.

 The closer you are to your team, the better you will be able to notice behavioural changes. The more you have an open dialogue with people, the greater the opportunity to hear about issues. If the conflict is with you, then this may give you an opportunity to resolve the conflict before it escalates and other people become involved.

Your reaction to someone disclosing that there's a problem is critical to the outcome. If you act defensively or trivialize a problem that's important to someone, you are likely to add fuel to the fire. If you act supportively and use negative feedback constructively, you are more likely to get a better outcome and make people more likely to disclose sensitive information in future.

## How to resolve conflict

Imagine that you have had a big argument with someone in your work or personal life. These five styles, based on work by Kenneth Thomas and Ralph Kilmann, are ways that you can handle the situation:

- **Avoid:** You decide just to ignore the issue and hope it goes away (lose–lose).

- **Compete:** You are adamant that you won't back down until you have got your own way, even if the other party is not happy (win–lose).

- **Accommodate:** You hate conflict, so you give in to the other party, even if it means forgoing your own needs (lose–win).

- **Compromise:** You reach an agreement whereby both parties are partly, but not completely, satisfied (win some, lose some).

- **Collaborate:** You are able to resolve the disagreement in such a way that both parties are highly satisfied with the outcome and have achieved what they wanted (win–win).

**THINK ABOUT IT**

1a) Which of the five conflict-handling styles do you think you use most often?

1b) How pleased are you with the outcome when you use this style?

2a) Think of five people you know who each regularly display one of the styles.

2b) How good is the outcome resulting from using each particular style?

3a) We've given you labels for each scenario, e.g. 'lose–lose', 'win–win'. Why has each strategy been given its particular label?

3b) How well do these labels match with the outcomes that you identified in step 2b?

---

The labels 'win–win', 'lose–win' etc. are just rules of thumb. There may be a situation where it's appropriate to avoid a confrontation – for example, if you know that you just need to calm down and the situation is likely to resolve itself. However, more often than not, you can get a better outcome if you aim to collaborate to solve an issue, than if you simply avoid it.

## Plan how you want a conflict to be resolved

Most of us will have a preferred style when it comes to conflict-handling. So when we face an argument, we don't often consciously sit down and think: 'There are five different ways I could approach this strategy – what are the pros and cons of using each one, and which will get the best outcome?'

Instead we might just walk out of the room or give in, because that's our way of dealing with conflict. It's therefore well worth being aware of your natural, unconscious behaviour when it comes to handling conflict and spending time considering which strategy is most appropriate for the situation you're in. If you're managing people who are in conflict, try to get them to do this too.

---

 When deciding which strategy to use, try to consider the importance of the relationship. If it's only a very short-term relationship then it may be appropriate to try to win what you want at all costs. However, if it's an important relationship, such as that between a manager and an employee, it's probably not helpful in the longer term to try to 'win' at their expense, in which case a 'collaborative' or 'compromise' solution may be more beneficial.

---

## Lessons from an orange

A wise lady called Mary Parker Follet told a great story about two sisters having a fight over an orange. There was only one orange, and both sisters needed one orange for their cooking.

---

 Think about the five different handling styles and consider how each can be applied to resolve the conflict between the two sisters. For example, if neither sister got to use the orange, this would be a 'lose–lose' scenario.

---

When posing this scenario to managers, they will often say that the compromise would be to cut the orange in half, and that collaborating would involve going to the shops and buying another orange! However, in business we are often fighting for finite resources, and we can't simply go out and buy another metaphorical orange. What is therefore nice about this story is the fact that if the sisters had taken the time to understand each other's needs, rather than immediately falling into conflict, they would have discovered that one sister wanted the *juice* of the orange and one wanted the *zest*.

## Negotiating to resolve conflict

In order for the sisters to have both got what they wanted, they would have needed to:

1. Know what they themselves wanted to achieve – the 'must haves', the 'ideal to haves' and the 'loss leaders' (i.e. what they were prepared to give up).

2. Know what strategy they wanted to aim for – e.g. win–win, win–lose.

3. Understand what the other party wanted – their 'musts', 'ideals' and 'loss leaders'.

4. Identify the negotiation elements – i.e. everything that could be bargained over.

5. Aim to reach a consensus.

When trying to resolve a conflict, be prepared to trade. This is why it's important to have all three categories of 'musts', 'ideals' and 'loss leaders' clearly defined from the start.

---

 A win–win approach starts by looking for solutions that meet all needs and moves backwards, gradually and only as far as necessary, towards compromise, to come up with a solution that meets as many needs as possible. It's usually better to aim high because it's difficult to trade up and easier to trade away concessions.

---

## When agreement still cannot be reached

When two parties are in conflict, it's usually best that they informally try to sort out the situation themselves, perhaps with the support of another person to mediate and help them find a solution using the steps outlined above.

If the negotiation fails and a solution still cannot be reached, sometimes it's necessary that an impartial third party listens to both sides of the arguments and makes a fair decision as to how the conflict will be resolved. As a manager, it may be appropriate that you take this decision. However, depending on the severity of the issue or how involved you are, you may need support from other parties such as your own manager, HR or an external body who can provide you with impartial advice.

This should, however, be a last resort – remember that most problems are not insurmountable and get resolved in the end.

---

 Quarrels and conflicts can be overcome by applying conflict-handling styles. During conflict-management, identify 'must haves' and what can be traded, aiming for a win–win solution whenever possible.

---

# R: Respect

*Never take a person's dignity: it is worth everything to them,
and nothing to you.*

Frank Barron

Sonia overheard her manager say that he had never seen anyone's face resemble a pepperoni pizza as much as Sonia's. He also embarrassed her by asking in a team meeting, 'Have you managed to trap a man yet?' – referring to her recent decision to try internet dating.

But the 'icing on the cake' happened recently, when he called her a 'paper pusher', by which he meant that she should do exactly what she was told, even if she didn't agree with it. Sonia, who has been a management consultant for the firm for many years and is close to qualifying with an MBA, was disgusted at the term 'paper pusher' and the sentiment behind it, feeling that her brain was not valued.

Interestingly, Sonia related this story in front of her friend Jeremy, who remarked: 'I told my team member today that she was just there to make me cups of tea and she found it funny. Ten minutes later a cup of tea had arrived on my desk.'

So what's the difference between telling someone they are just there to make cups of tea, and that they are just there to do what they are told? Looking at it on paper, perhaps not all that much. Yet these two circumstances led to very different emotional outcomes. Sometimes these comments are fine, other times they leave people feeling totally disrespected.

## So what's the difference that makes the difference?

Firstly, it comes down to the outlook of the person on the receiving end of the comments. Some people might take the comment about whether they have 'trapped a man' as harmless banter, whereas others could be extremely offended by it. There can be a fine line between energizing office banter and insulting behaviour.

**REMEMBER THIS!!!** As a manager, you need to ensure that you are accurately judging whether your team members will find your comments and behaviour acceptable. If in doubt, the rule of thumb says that you err on the side of caution and resist making potentially offensive comments.

If you are making comments like this in public, you also need to take into account how other people overhearing the comments might feel – you really have to take this seriously.

For example, in Chapter K: 'Kindness' we described how an employee broke down one day because her father was undergoing gender reassignment and she was struggling to come to terms with this. Over the past few months, she had been repeatedly been distressed by 'harmless office banter' about 'men in skirts', which was clearly anything but funny to this particular individual.

Secondly, it comes down to what you are saying. If you are speaking words with some truth behind them, then first of all you should consider whether they actually need to be said. It was not Sonia's manager's job to comment on her skin condition. However, if some work-related feedback does need to be given, for example if someone is being argumentative to a point that it's unhelpful, then you should consider how you can deliver the message in a way that doesn't make them lose respect for you or feel insulted. Remember that some more tips on how to do this were included in Chapter F: 'Feedback'.

---

 You are managing someone who repeatedly makes stupid mistakes that are going to be a hassle for you to sort out. Is it acceptable to shout at that person? What is the justification for your answer?

We were running a training course preparing managers for this type of scenario and one manager argued that sometimes you need to take people aside and give them a 'bit of a b*llocking', albeit in private. It was fascinating to see a well-respected and very senior manager quickly step in and make it very clear that no matter who you are, who you are managing or what they have done, it is *never* acceptable to give anyone 'a bit of a b*llocking' in public or in private.

---

When interviewing people about what makes a good and bad manager, time after time, our interviewees have made a link between managers failing to treat people respectfully and this behaviour having a negative impact on those who experience and witness it.

For example, Mike described how he had the interesting experience of working for two managers at the same time, allowing him to evaluate the impact that their differing management styles had upon him. One manager shouted at him and told him what to do. The other had a much more collaborative and trusting approach. Mike didn't enjoy his job as much when he was reporting to the person who shouted at him, and avoided going to him with problems, finding the other manager far more approachable. Interestingly, Mike concluded that he worked equally hard for both managers, and the experience taught him that you don't need to 'whack people' to make them do well. And now that he's a manager he's still of this belief and uses it to guide his own behaviour, no matter how frustrating the situation!

Research reveals that Mike's more aggressive manager was actually quite lucky that Mike worked equally hard for him.

---

 Professor Christine Pearson, co-author of *The Cost of Bad Behavior*, found that 50% of people decrease their effort at work after experiencing ongoing rude behaviour. It's not just people's feelings that are impacted by disrespectful treatment: it can influence an organization's bottom line.

---

Interestingly, Pearson also found that 60% of disrespectful treatment in the workplace comes from people more senior than you, 20% from a peer and 20% from subordinates.

## When disrespectful behaviour goes too far

When managers cross the boundaries of acceptable behaviour, they can be subject to accusations of bullying. Bullying often involves a person in authority repeatedly abusing their position and exerting their dominance to produce circumstances that create a health and safety risk, both physical and mental. However, an individual may also bully a peer, and there are cases of people bullying their line manager.

Sadly, workplace bullying is all too common, with 93% of HR practitioners reporting that bullying occurs in their own organizations (according to the Andrea Adams Trust).

The following are a number of non-verbal and verbal examples of behaviour that could be considered as bullying:

**Non-verbal**

- Regularly undermining a person's professional or personal standing.
- Regularly picking on one person in front of others.
- Unnecessarily monitoring somebody's work or intrusively doing so.
- Deliberately seeking to make somebody appear incompetent.
- Taking away areas of responsibility without discussing it first or providing any notification.
- Unfairly preventing someone from receiving a promotion.
- Deliberately concealing information or providing somebody with incorrect information.
- Deliberately overloading somebody with work.
- Intentional sabotage of a person's work.
- Aggressive body posture, gestures or physical contact.
- Direct physical intimidation, violence or attack.

**Verbal**

- Humiliating somebody through constant innuendo, belittling them or putting them down.
- Personal insults and name-calling.
- Persistently threatening someone over their job security.
- Making false accusations about someone.

- Repeatedly shouting, screaming or swearing at a person, in public or in private.
- Direct verbal intimidation, violence or attack.

Managers should avoid displaying all of the behaviours described above and should take complaints of bullying from their team members seriously, seeking advice from their HR department or manager should this occur. You should also advise any member of your team displaying this type of behaviour that it's completely unacceptable and could lead to dismissal. Do not underestimate the impact that bullying can have on a person's life and your responsibility in preventing this from happening.

---

 **IF YOU REMEMBER ONE THING** Managers have a responsibility to staff to create a safe workplace founded upon respect and free from bullying and harassment of any kind.

---

# S: Strengths

*Never try to teach a pig to sing; it wastes your time and it annoys the pig.*

Paul Dickson

Everyone has strengths and weaknesses. This chapter explores the differences between them, and the benefits of a person playing to their strengths.

However, first we'll explore when it's OK for someone to ignore their weaknesses and when it isn't.

---

 Think back to your time at school. What subjects were you naturally really good at? What subjects just weren't for you?

---

Some students are amazing artists; others are brilliant at chemistry. Some have an astounding talent for maths, while others are talented at speaking foreign languages. And while some people seem to be brilliant at virtually everything, most of us aren't quite so fortunate. We find that there are some things that make us feel like a square peg in a round hole. For example, despite several attempts at learning various instruments during my childhood, I've never mastered the art of reading music. My brain would much rather *hear* the notes and try to replicate them than look at funny black dots on the page. Yet to musicians reading music must seem so simple.

## Can you learn to do things that you aren't naturally good at?

In some respects the answer to this question is 'yes'. If I sat down every day for the next ten years and tried to read music, I'm sure I'd be able to succeed. Psychologist Anders Ericsson found that there was only one factor that differentiated average students from outstanding ones at Berlin's elite Academy of Music: the amount that the students practised.

---

 You will probably know from your own experience that there are many things that we *can* learn to do if we try. This means that when deciding whether or not to put the effort in, you need to ask yourself: 'Am I motivated to improve?' and 'Does it actually matter if I can't do this?'

---

Although I probably could learn to read music, when it comes to the question of, 'Should I put the effort in to do this', the answer is 'no'. In the context of my current life, it doesn't actually matter in the slightest whether I can read music or not. So it may be a 'flaw', but it isn't what I would call a 'fatal flaw'.

## When is a flaw a 'fatal flaw'?

To explore this question further, let's take another example. I'll also admit to being one of those people who always had 'Could improve at spelling' written on my school reports. I've since realized that, just as I try to play music by ear, my brain prefers to spell phonetically. Looking at this in the context of my work, accurate spelling is actually *highly* important in written communication. Yet it isn't a 'fatal flaw' because of computer spell-checkers, editors and proof-readers. However, if I was a professional proofreader then this would be a 'fatal flaw'.

## But should we try to improve 'fatal flaws'?

In Chapters F: 'Feedback' and G: 'Goal-setting', we talked about the benefits of letting people know how they are doing against the objectives that they have been set. If you aren't performing against fundamental aspects of your job, then this is a problem that requires addressing – for example, by employing the approach outlined in the next chapter, T: 'Training'.

---

 When a flaw is 'fatal', then yes, action needs to be taken. Even when something isn't a 'fatal flaw', it's still useful to get feedback on it as a potential development area.

---

There's no getting away from it: feedback on your 'developmental areas' is very important, as is resolving a situation when you *do* have a fatal flaw. This can be done either through working hard to improve it, or by finding a way to no longer have to do this aspect of work as part of your role.

## But I'd rather play to my strengths

And this is the crux of our chapter. What would you rather do, given the choice between:

(a) Something that you aren't very good at and that bores you rigid; and

(b) Something that you genuinely enjoy and you are able to do well?

Certainly, if you gave me the choice between designing a management training course or proofreading it, the first option would be the hands-down winner.

So, thinking of 'strengths' as things that you are good at and enjoy doing, what are the benefits of playing to your strengths at work? Marcus Buckingham and Donald Clifton share some great research (completed by the Gallup Organization) in their book, *Now, Discover Your Strengths*. After studying 200,000 employees in 36 different companies, Gallup found that people who strongly agree that they have the opportunity to play to their strengths every day were:

- 38% more likely to work in more productive business units;
- 44% more likely to work in business areas with higher customer satisfaction scores;
- 50% more likely to work in a business area with lower employee turnover.

So aside from enjoying your work more, there are some tangible business benefits to playing to your strengths.

Look back at your answer(s) to question 'S' from Chapter A: 'Assessment', which asked:

- 'My manager enables me to play to my strengths at work' (Rating of your own manager)
- 'I enable my team to play to their strengths in their work' (Rating of yourself as a manager)

If you were able to strongly agree to these questions (i.e. rated 5 out of 5), your organization would be likely to reap the benefits as listed above from the Gallup Organization's research.

## How can people identify what their strengths are, and play to them more?

There are various psychometric tools available that can help people to identify their strengths. If you'd like to find out more about these, go to: www.management-handbook.com

In the meantime, an easy place to start is to simply ask yourself the question: 'What are my strengths at work?'

1.  Make a list of as many things as you can that you are good at. (Examples might be doing presentations, researching on the internet or doing sales calls. If you get stuck, ask people who know you well what they think you are really good at, and think about work that has gone really well in the past and positive feedback that you have been given.)

2.  Tick the things on the list that you really enjoy doing. You should consider these to be your strengths.

3.  Circle the things on the list that you do regularly as part of your current job.

4.  For anything that you have circled, brainstorm ways that you can make use of this strength more in your current role. Pick the number one thing that you would like to do, in order to play to your strengths more.

5.  For anything that you have ticked, brainstorm ways that you can make use of this strength more in your future career. Pick the number one thing that you would like to do, in order to play to your strengths more.

6.  Share your strengths (and your 'number one' things) with your team and manager.

7.  Ask them to remember you when a task that plays to your strengths arises in future.

You can also use this exercise with your team members to help them identify and play to their strengths.

## Why sharing and playing to your strengths can improve teamwork

Dr Meredith Belbin proposed that there are nine different roles in a team, including: a 'Plant' who is great at coming up with ideas; a 'Resource Investigator' who is good at going out and finding the information and resources needed by the team; and a 'Completer Finisher' who ensures that the 'loose ends' of a task are tied up and the job is completed to a high standard.

Belbin's Team Role Theory proposes that people within the team will have strengths in different areas and, critically, that individuals should be given opportunities to play to those strengths, since each of the nine roles is important to the team's success.

For example, it doesn't matter how good your idea is (the Plant), or how much research you can gather to back it up (Resource Investigator) if your team constantly gets distracted by the next opportunity and no one finishes the job (Completer Finisher). In addition, giving the right people the right tasks is critical to overall success. Asking a Plant to ensure a polished finish might not lead to a great result, whereas a Completer Finisher might thrive at the same task.

---

 When planning work, always consider how to play to the strengths of your team. One idea of work-hell might be someone else's idea of work-heaven – so work smarter, not harder, and as long as you're fair and everyone is happy (remember Chapter J: 'Justice'), it can have a really positive impact for the team as a whole and for individuals within it.

---

 Wherever possible, focus on identifying strengths in yourself and among team members and play to them – individuals, teams and organizations will reap the benefits as a result.

---

# T: Training

*It's all to do with the training: you can do a lot if you're properly trained.*

HM Queen Elizabeth II

There are three key reasons why individuals and teams need training:

1. To enable them to carry out the **basic functions** of their job.
2. To support **performance improvement** once the basic functions of the job have been mastered.
3. To **motivate and reward** individuals who want to feel that they are developing personally and professionally.

Since training plays a key role in enabling employees to perform at their best, and companies spend a lot of money investing in it, it's critical that people get the right training. Managers play a key role in identifying training opportunities. Specifically, they must be able to identify:

- When training is required.
- How a person/team will benefit.
- Precisely what trainees need to know or do differently after training.
- What the right training solution is to achieve the desired outcome.

If this process (called **training needs analysis**) sounds a little daunting, don't worry. We've broken it down into six simple questions to help you. We'll give you the questions first and provide an example of how they can be applied.

## The six steps of training needs analysis

To understand what training your team (or members of it) need, ask the following questions:

### Step 1: The need or opportunity

What is the business case for training and development?

### Step 2: Consequences

What are the negative consequences of failing to address the need (or seize the opportunity)?

### Step 3: Future

How would you like the person/team to perform in the future?

### Step 4: Barriers

What is preventing the person/team from being where they need to be?

### Step 5: Gap

What are the skills, knowledge, attitude and behavioural deficiencies?

## Step 6: Solution

Can these deficiencies be filled by a training intervention? If so, what is the most appropriate type?

For your convenience, a template containing these questions can be downloaded from the website www.management-handbook.com

---

 This six-step process can be used:

- For *any* of the three training purposes outlined at the beginning of the chapter (basic role training, performance improvement, and motivation/reward).
- To identify *individual* training needs as well as the needs of a *whole team*.

---

## Training needs analysis in action

Let's return to the case study of Jean from Chapter P: 'Poor performance', who had to go through the formal performance improvement plan. Let's see how the six-step process outlined above could have supported Jean to improve.

## Step 1: The need or opportunity

Jean had been classified as 'under-performing' in her annual appraisal. This was largely because she was repeatedly failing to meet her deadlines and was unable to take on a comparable volume of work to other team members.

## Step 2: Consequences
- External customers were unhappy, as their deadlines were not being met.
- The other members of the team felt annoyed/pressured by having to take on additional work to compensate for Jean's share.
- According to company policy, Jean faced possible dismissal if she was unable to improve her performance.
- Jean was suffering from stress, as she felt overloaded with work.

## Step 3: Future
Jean's manager wanted to see her:

- Meeting deadlines.
- Being able to take on as much volume of work as other team members.
- Feeling less stressed and more in control.

## Step 4: Barriers
The barriers that were preventing desired performance included:

- Jean's constant desire for total perfection, which dramatically slowed her down.

- Jean's reliance upon other people to give her information in order to complete her own work. However, they were not giving this information to her on time. She did chase people for information, but only a couple of days after she actually needed it.

- Jean's mind-set that it wasn't her fault that she couldn't meet her deadlines (it was because other people weren't meeting hers), which meant that she took the attitude: 'If it's late, it's late.'

- Facing a vicious circle – the more behind Jean got with one project, the further back it pushed her work on other projects, and she was constantly playing catch-up.

## Step 5: Gap
- **Knowledge**: Jean needed to know how 'good' is 'good enough' in the eyes of the organization.

- **Skills**: Jean needed to be able to plan deadlines, identifying what information was needed by when, including contingency time.

- **Attitude:** Jean needed to take on a new mind-set that it wasn't OK to miss deadlines.

- **Behaviour**: Jean needed to become more assertive and proactive when chasing people to supply her with information.

**Step 6: Solution**

- What types of training interventions could have helped Jean to improve her knowledge, skills, attitude and behaviour?
- Are there any non-training-based solutions that would help Jean to improve (e.g. stop giving new work to Jean until she had totally caught up, then start again with a clean slate)?

For suggested answers as to what might have helped Jean to improve, see www.management-handbook.com. Remember that to solve a situation, you don't always need to throw training at the problem, so always consider which non-training solutions might help.

In this real-life case study, one of the key reasons why Jean's performance failed to improve was because she was given the wrong training (an emotional intelligence course). Although this course may have helped her to appear more in control, it didn't do enough to address the root cause of the problems: her perfectionism, poor time management and lack of proactive behaviour.

If your recommended training interventions aren't having the desired impact upon members of your team, you should ask yourself: 'Have I chosen the right intervention?' Their performance is, after all, a reflection of your management capability.

---

## What types of training solution are available?

Although most of us think of training as learning from a teacher sitting in a classroom, training can take many other forms, for example:

1. On-the-job learning (receiving feedback as you do your actual job).
2. Shadowing a peer (watching how a colleague does their job).
3. Self-directed learning (where the learner chooses what resources to use, e.g. what books to read).
4. E-learning training courses (where a person learns via a computer-based training programme).
5. Mentoring (where a person has access to an experienced individual who can pass on their expertise and advice).

---

 There's more than one form of training. Part of selecting the right training solution involves selecting the right **content** (i.e. what is learnt). The other part involves selecting the right **method** (i.e. how the person learns). Always try to think of what type of training solution will be most effective for the situation at hand.

---

## How do you get buy-in from the person and identify a solution?

Imagine that you are Jean's manager. What is the difference between:

(a) Telling her what you have decided as a result of going through the training needs analysis steps 1–6 on her behalf; and

(b) Working though the six steps with her, getting her to identify as many of the answers as she can?

It's always best to work collaboratively with individuals in your team to identify their training needs. If they can self-identify how they can improve and can suggest ways of doing this, there will be a number of benefits, including the fact that they are more likely to have buy-in to the solutions chosen than if they are simply told they have to do something, Collaborative training needs analysis may also help you to choose the right training solutions, as individuals themselves will have better insight into what they need and want, and how they best like to learn.

## Ensuring the benefits of training are realized

One of the biggest failings of training is that no one checks to see whether the person is actually implementing or benefiting from what they learnt during the process.

A very important managerial role is to be aware of what training your team members have experienced and to follow up, perhaps a month later, to determine what positive difference the training has made. If the training was worth the investment in the first place, it's worth following up on its impact.

---

 Where there's a need or an opportunity for a change in skill, knowledge, attitude or behaviour, the correct form of training can provide a solution as long as it's correctly applied.

---

# U: Upward progression

*When I was younger I used to get frustrated that I wasn't*
*getting promoted fast enough. With hindsight, I realize that*
*I was actually being promoted at the right pace.*

Roy, advertising industry

Looking back on my own career, I can empathize with Roy. During my twenties, like many others, I was hungry for the next step in my career and was prepared to work exceptionally hard to achieve it. But I can also see what a complete pain I must have been for my managers. As soon as I had been promoted, I was always aiming for the next step up the ladder. I pushed and pushed for promotions, leading to three of them within the space of four years, and my manager was understandably running out of options. There was no obvious next step, other than her job – and there were lots of other people in the queue for that, plus she wasn't planning on leaving anyway.

In situations like this, highly enthusiastic employees who strive to do a great job can become very demotivated and think about leaving. Managers become frustrated because they feel that their hands are tied, and perhaps that their team members' expectations are unrealistic. To top it off, under tough economic conditions there may also be a lack of resources to distribute to people. Whereas there might previously have been some budget to pacify an individual, for example paying for them to gain a new qualification, for many organizations those financial wells have now dried up.

So what can managers do to keep team members feeling like they are developing and progressing, while managing their expectations within the constraints that they are under?

---

**THINK ABOUT IT** Imagine that you were my former manager. Think of different ways that you could have handled my desire to keep learning and developing. What would be your recommended solution to overcome this issue?

---

What actually happened was that, with genuinely good intentions, nothing concrete ever materialized. I was told there was a possible promotion opportunity in the pipeline, I just had to wait six months, then another six months – but eighteen months later this was never realized. Eventually I was told that there was nothing that the organization could do to help me progress. If I didn't feel satisfied, then I should try to find a job elsewhere. The manager may have been trying to be truthful and helpful, but it was a very demotivating message to hear.

In the end there was a solution, which worked really well. The head of my department allowed me to reduce my working hours from five days to three days per week.

- The team benefited from keeping access to a skill-set that the organization had invested in, and from retaining an experienced team member with good organizational contacts who was well placed to just get on and do the job.

- Management benefited from lowering the overall head-count of the team, which was beneficial at a time of organizational cutbacks.

- I benefited from being able to satisfy my hunger for progression by having two days a week to begin developing my own business, yet retaining the security of a steady, albeit smaller, income from my organization. I felt privileged to have been given this opportunity and worked really hard on the three days per week that I continued to do my existing role.

If we link back to the conflict-handling styles covered in Chapter Q: 'Quarrels', my management team and I were able to find a win–win solution to a difficult problem.

I have since tried to think of other solutions that might have worked in this situation. With hindsight I can see that organizations can frequently miss a trick when it comes to developing individuals. Without spending additional money, there are lots of things that you can do to make people feel like they are developing. Here are a few ideas.

---

- **Create exposure to senior management activities within their team:** If someone has ambitions for senior management, even though they may be some way away, make a list of all of the things that senior managers do, and over the course of a year or two, give them opportunities to tick off shadowing opportunities on the list. For example, when you're preparing the departmental budget, take half an hour to show your team member how you did it. It's good to share this type of knowledge, as you're passing on important information to potential future leaders.

- **Make someone a deputy manager:** For someone looking to progress into a managerial role for the first time, being able to say on your résumé that you have been a deputy manager can really help and can enhance a person's feelings of status and self-esteem. It can be helpful to you as a manager to have a member of the team who can 'keep the ship sailing' when you are on annual leave, for example by attending meetings on your behalf. When using this strategy, be creative when there's more than one person who would like to gain managerial experience, and make sure you don't just dump work you don't want to do on your deputy. Gaining experience of a managerial admin task is one thing, but doing the same boring tasks over and over again doesn't motivate people or help them to learn.

- **Promote access to a mentor:** It can be very motivating for an employee to meet a mentor for, say, one hour every month, to discuss anything and everything – such as how the mentor managed to climb the ranks, or how to handle conflict. It can be helpful for managers and senior managers to help junior employees to identify a suitable mentor, as they may not have the organizational knowledge/contacts to do this themselves. In terms of career development, a mentor who works outside of the individual's team can be more helpful in maintaining confidentiality about things discussed, removing conflicts of interest, and providing a different perspective.

- **Secondments within other business areas:** Having the opportunity to work on short-term projects can be extremely motivating and beneficial to employees. It can give them a break from their normal work, and they can learn new skills and make helpful organizational contacts. When offering secondments, management need to ensure that they can cover the existing workload of the team without putting unacceptable additional burden on the other members, and that access to secondment opportunities is fair.

---

Activities like these can help to prepare individuals for a specific role, or can give them useful advanced skills such as how to develop a project strategy, which is relevant to a wide variety of roles if an actual career path isn't yet obvious.

## The importance of managing people's expectations

When using these types of development activities, you must be careful to manage the expectations of your team members. You cannot promise them a promotion. However, at the same time you must demonstrate that you are serious about putting people in the best possible position to be selected should an opportunity arise.

---

Roy said that one of the most difficult discussions in his managerial career was when he had to manage the expectations of a team member, John, who had been working very hard because he wanted to be promoted. John had been set six very clear objectives that he needed to demonstrate in order to be promoted to the next level, but in Roy's opinion, John still needed to improve on two out of the six areas. Roy said it was particularly tough since John was his friend, and he made the comment that, 'More often than not, your own perception of how you are doing is better than everyone else's.'

Roy had to take the tough decision to tell John that he could not be promoted, and John was very unhappy about this decision.

Simply managing someone's expectations by saying that they aren't ready can lead to a negative outcome, perhaps with them looking for a new job. Telling someone they aren't good enough is not a great message to hear. But Roy was able to achieve a really positive outcome, so how did he do it?

1. Roy inspired John to feel that although he wasn't ready now, that didn't mean that he couldn't do it. Roy wanted John to believe that it was worth it to keep trying hard.

2.  Roy helped John to clearly understand the gap in his performance and to define the required standard.

3.  Roy genuinely offered every support that he could give to help John meet his two final objectives.

The result was that John worked extremely hard for the next six months, at which point his performance had improved sufficiently that he met the criteria for the promotion.

---

When a promotion is important to someone, helping them to progress at a fast enough pace can be very challenging, particularly if your hands feel tied – for example, if you don't have the authority to make that decision. In this situation, always try to focus on what you *can* do (rather than what you *can't*) to support the person to be in the best possible position so that when the time is right, they are well placed for promotion. If they don't know what they want to do next, think of ways that you can expose them to learning about other opportunities, such as meeting with other members of the organization to find out about their roles.

---

 A manager can't promise a promotion but can do their best to help a person to be promotion-ready.

---

# V: Values

*Just as your car runs more smoothly and requires less energy to go faster and farther when the wheels are in perfect alignment, you perform better when your thoughts, feelings, emotions, goals, and values are in balance.*

Brian Tracy

Did you know that employees (like all people) are like onions? No, not because they can make you want to cry at times, but because we all have multiple layers …

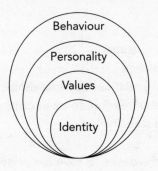

At the heart of our onion is our **identity**. This consists of 'I am' statements, such as:

- I am 35 years old.
- I am male.
- I am a doctor.
- I am a parent.
- I am a home-owner.

You can probably see from the list above that aspects to do with our identities describe the fundamental components of our lives.

The next layer is our **values**. Our values can be shaped by our identity – for example, if we are a parent, we may value financial stability to support our family. Our values are also shaped by our experience and upbringing. For instance, some people will be naturally risk-averse – they value security, a value passed on from our parents. Overall, values should be considered as things that are really important to you. Work-related examples might include how much we value:

- Money
- Visible signs of status
- Life–work balance
- Close working relationships/friendships with colleagues
- Autonomy (the freedom to be in control yourself)
- Security and stability
- Learning
- Hedonism (the desire to have fun in life).

Our values are closely related to our **personality**. The things that are important to us shape the way that we behave. For example, if we value autonomy, this is likely to show up in a personality preference of working independently. Examples of aspects of our personality include:

- How extraverted we are

- How calm we are
- How much we plan and how organized we are
- How assertive we are
- How serious we are
- How private we are.

We will look at the implications of these personality factors in Chapter Y: 'Your personality'.

Finally, the outer layer of our onion is our **behaviour** – and just like the skin of an onion, it's what you see. Our behaviour is influenced by our identity, values and personality.

---

Think about how your own identity, values and personality influence the way that you behave.

---

## So why are values so important?

Values are close to the core of a person. They are the things that drive us and have a powerful effect on our behaviour. For example, someone who values stability will be likely to react badly to serious, negative organizational change compared to someone who doesn't particularly value stability.

**REMEMBER THIS!!!**

Clearly your identity also has a role to play here. For example, if you are a home-owner with a mortgage to pay, you may react differently to a threat of redundancy compared to someone who is living with their parents. However, values themselves have a strong influence on our behaviour: you could have two people in exactly the same life circumstance, with one valuing security and stability and the other not so much, and you could have a very different reaction to the same organizational change.

When we value something, several things happen:

- We will behave in a way that is conducive to us satisfying the value; e.g. if we value money, we are likely to seek opportunities to increase our pay.

- We feel demotivated when we can't satisfy that value; e.g. if we value autonomy, we can feel very frustrated when we aren't allowed to be in control of our own work.

- We will tend to have better working relationships with people who value the same things as us; e.g. if we value hedonism, we are likely to thrive working with people who also enjoy creating a sense of fun while at work.

So values are intrinsically linked to our behaviour, satisfaction with work, motivation and working relationships.

## Do values change?

The answer to this question is 'not much'. Our values can change if a major life event happens to us. For example, someone who previously greatly valued status in their life (and always needed to be seen with the latest mobile phone or driving a nice car) could change dramatically following a cancer scare. Suddenly the material aspects that seemed so important cease to matter so much. Similarly, hedonistic people who were out all night in their late teens can value a quieter life once they become a parent. So priorities can change. However, most of the time, our values remain quite stable. Unless anything major happens, we aren't likely to suddenly wake up one morning and love learning when we haven't ever been interested in it before.

## Why are values so important to managers?

We said above that values have a powerful influence on a person's behaviour and can leave them feeling highly motivated when values are satisfied, or demotivated when they are not. There are some things that will motivate or demotivate virtually everyone: the vast majority of people would not enjoy being verbally abused at work. However, when it comes to values, the amount that they motivate or demotivate will differ from person to person.

**THINK ABOUT IT**

Let's take two people doing the same job. Person A isn't motivated by money at all, but loves learning. Person B doesn't care whether they learn or not, so long as their pay keeps increasing.

- How would person A react to the opportunity to gain a new qualification, which won't increase their salary?
- How would person B react to the opportunity to gain a new qualification, which won't increase their salary?
- How would person A react to being told that there's no budget for personal development this year, but they will get a pay rise?
- How would person B react to being told that there's no budget for personal development this year, but they will get a pay rise?

From this exercise you will see that giving two people with different values the same treatment can lead to different reactions. As a manager, you need to take time to understand what is important to people – and wherever possible, while still being fair to everyone, strive to satisfy those values. For example, if someone values learning, aim to allow them time during the week to work on a qualification or skill. If another individual values hedonism, allow them the same amount of time to get involved with activities such as organizing department team-building events. It's amazing what a big difference these seemingly small strategies can make.

## We don't need to be treated the same

In Chapter J: 'Justice' we talked about the importance of treating people fairly. However, it's very important to note that this doesn't mean treating people *the same*.

---

Amanda works just one day per week as part of a great team. Her team-mates, who really value close working relationships and teamwork, make a real effort to organize all team events on the days that she is in.

Although Amanda really appreciates her colleagues' desire to include her, she doesn't mind either way if she is included or not. She doesn't particularly value hedonism, so she doesn't mind if she misses out on team drinks, and would rather spend her limited time focusing on getting her work done rather than attending team-building events.

Amanda had a word with her manager to say that she's very happy for team meetings and events to take place on days when she isn't in, as she gets real enjoyment from simply doing her work. Since relations are good between Amanda and the team, she is quite capable of keeping herself informed, so everyone is fine with Amanda not attending every team event.

---

## We see the world through our own glasses

You may well have looked at person A in the activity just now and thought: 'They're nuts, how can anyone value learning over money?' Equally, other people may not relate to person B. When you value something strongly, it can be really difficult to comprehend why it isn't important to everyone.

You can think of this as viewing the world through your own glasses. You see the world a certain way, but other people have different glasses. You shouldn't assume that the things that are important to you will be as important to other people. Similarly, you shouldn't assume that the things that are unimportant to you don't matter to others. Just because you're happy to stay at work late in the hope that you'll get that promotion, it doesn't mean that someone else wouldn't rather be at home with their family. As a manager, you have to learn to take your own glasses off and try to put other people's on, no matter how odd the view looks.

 Think about times when your managers have supported you to achieve the things that are important to you – and how they found this out in the first place.

As a manager yourself, you can simply ask people in a 1:1 meeting what is important to them and say that you will try to meet their needs wherever you can.

## What if I can't satisfy someone's needs?

As a manager, you can't keep all people happy all of the time. But it's important to do your best to meet people's needs. Try to be creative in the way you manage people, playing deliberately to the things that really matter to individuals. If you really can't help them to achieve what they want, then it's important to manage their expectations and accept and be supportive of the fact that they need to find another path. Remember that people's values are strong and are unlikely to go away. But it will help people to know that they have your genuine support.

---

 Our values underlie our personality and our behaviour. Everybody's will be different, so as a manager it's important you understand what these are and find ways to satisfy them.

---

# W: Well done

*Appraisals are where you get together with your team leader
and agree what an outstanding member of the team you are,
how much your contribution has been valued, what massive
potential you have and, in recognition of all this, would you
mind having your salary halved.*

Theodore Roosevelt

---

Louisa's manager Sara could clearly see that Louisa had worked phenomenally hard that year. Louisa had run a highly successful, one-day seminar 94 times in twelve months, while her two closest peers had run it only 51 times between them. Why the discrepancy in numbers? Because Louisa was so good at her job that her services were constantly in demand from her customers.

Running the seminar meant a start time of 8.00am for Louisa, and she often didn't finish clearing up until 6.00pm. This meant that Louisa was doing approximately three hours of overtime every day that she ran the course, in addition to her contracted seven-hour work day. Over the course of the year, she'd done many more hours than anyone else in the team.

Sara also recognized that Louisa's job had required her to spend much of the year living in a hotel. Louisa had often commented to Sara how much she disliked sitting on her own in a hotel room, night after night, missing out on her social life back home.

Understandably, Sara was more than happy to recognize Louisa's effort in her annual performance review. She felt that Louisa really deserved the top bonus in the team. There was only a limited pot of money to go around, and the benchmark for acceptable performance had been set at a 6% bonus. However, Louisa was going to be awarded double this amount to reflect her outstanding performance.

Sara also intended to praise and thank Louisa for her work, and tell her that she was fantastic compared to her peers at delivering the seminar.

---

So, great feedback and a top bonus – what a winning combination to create a motivated employee! Or was it?

It's time to do some maths on Louisa's 'recognition'.

---

- Louisa's salary before her bonus was £35,000 per year, so her 12% bonus equated to £4,200 additional pay that year.

- If Louisa's performance had merely been acceptable, she would have received a 6% bonus and therefore £2,100. The difference between acceptable and outstanding performance therefore equated to £2,100, which after government deductions of, say, 30%, leaves us with £1,470.

- Louisa did a total of 230 working days that year, which

means that on average, she earned an additional £6.39 per day for being a 'top performer'.

So ask yourself, for £6.39 extra per day, is it really worth working so much harder than everyone else?

---

This was a question Louisa asked herself following her performance review. Everyone in the team had received a bonus of 6% or more, yet Louisa realized that other people in the team were getting away with doing far less work and hours than she was: late starts, early finishes and long lunches. Plus no one had done overnight stays, or run as many tedious seminars as she had.

Also, while Louisa had been off-site running the same course over and over again she hadn't progressed much professionally. In contrast, her peers had had the opportunity to work on a variety of different projects that had grown and stretched them. Some of them had been on seminars themselves and had gained new qualifications, while Louisa had had no training opportunities in the last twelve months.

To make matters worse, Louisa had already been told that there was little prospect of her being promoted any time soon as there simply was no position to promote her to.

## The other side of reward and recognition

Louisa's manager would have been very shocked to hear that, far from her reward and recognition being highly motivating, Louisa became totally complacent following her performance review.

Louisa made a conscious decision that she would do the bare minimum she could get away with. She deliberately never volunteered to take on additional work like she used to (someone else could pick it up for a change!), and just like her peers, she began to come in late and go home earlier and get out of doing overnight trips whenever she could. The star of the team had decided that she could no longer be bothered to shine.

And sadly, no one really noticed the difference. The following year, after doing the bare minimum, Louisa was still awarded a bonus of 10% and was praised lavishly for her achievements, reinforcing the fact that there really was no point in trying.

So, is the impact of pay upon motivation and performance all it's cracked up to be? Here are some interesting facts that shed light on the matter:

- Money is a surprisingly ineffective motivator. Why? Because salary is a 'hygiene' factor, as we saw in Chapter B: 'Basics'. Knowing that you are getting paid every day doesn't typically make you jump up and down for joy in the office or rush to be at your desk at 7.00am – you simply expect to be paid, yet you feel disgruntled when you don't think you are being paid fairly, or experience a pay cut.

- Performance-related pay *can* motivate people to work hard but you have to make sure that there's an obvious link between effort and reward, and that the size of the reward is perceived to be worth the extra effort. When this doesn't happen, performance-related pay can fail to motivate people. Astonishingly, during the research for this book we met someone who was paid over £50,000 a year yet was barely 'lukewarm' about the fact that she expected to get a 100% bonus this year. Why? Because she got a 100% bonus every year, as did everyone else, even though she performed better than others.

- During the worldwide recession in 2008–09, research by the Corporate Leadership Council revealed that because there was less money to go around in bonuses, many managers typically tried to give a little bit of bonus to everyone. The impact of this was that the top performers began to try less hard and their productivity dropped – ironically, at the very time their efforts were required the most. The researchers concluded that, even if it isn't possible to reward people with money (because there simply isn't any) then managers have to find other non-monetary ways to reward and recognize top performers, otherwise they will become complacent.

Sometimes as a manager, your hands are tied. For example, you'd love to give everyone a healthy budget for personal development or a nice chunky bonus, but perhaps you're in the middle of a recession, or your company policies/budgets simply won't allow it. So what can you do to reward and recognize people, in a way that actually works?

---

 Imagine that you are Louisa's manager. Think carefully about how you could reward and recognize her, using realistic ways that will really make a positive difference to her, remembering that praise wasn't enough.

- When doing this, try to work out what will motivate Louisa and think of how to tap into this. Remember that you will have a more positive impact if you can reward and recognize a person in a way that best suits their preferences.

- Try to think of as many effective non-monetary solutions as possible, such as opportunities to work from home, or flexible hours.

---

## Distribution and frequency of recognition and reward

Ask yourself:

- If you never said 'thank you' to your team member, would this be enough?
- If you said 'thank you' every hour, would this be too often?

So when and how should we do it?

Firstly, think about how excited and pleased you feel to receive a Christmas card. Now think about how much *more* excited and pleased you would feel at receiving essentially the same thing, a piece of printed card in an envelope, but just randomly sent during the year by a friend to say something nice. Using this analogy, people may expect to be thanked at their annual appraisal, or at a team meeting. But think about how much more motivating it is to thank and reward people when they don't expect it.

---

Now think about how much more powerful it is to reward someone when there's something specific that really deserves recognition. Remember that specific and timely recognition reinforces the fact that their achievements are noticed and rewarded, and that their effort is worth it.

---

Finally, imagine that you received a card from a relative and an identical card, but this time sent personally by the President of the United States. Which one would make you feel more excited? A great tip that we heard from a manager is that he passes on details of really exceptional performance to the head of his company, who will personally come round and thank the individual concerned.

## Rewarding barely acceptable performance

Finally, should you reward people whose performance is barely acceptable? If someone's performance is barely acceptable and you reward them, then this reinforces the fact that this performance is OK, when really there's considerable room for improvement.

On the other hand, if you don't recognize what a person has done, then you risk demotivating them and causing their performance to deteriorate further.

---

A good tip is to recognize and reward the things that you would like to see more of. In psychological terms this is known as **positive reinforcement**.

---

For example, if someone is trying hard but achieving poor results, reward their effort. If someone is verging on not doing enough working hours, but is producing good work when they are there, reward their output. Make sure that when you do this, you are specific about what you are rewarding – you don't want to accidentally 'positively reinforce' the wrong thing. Linking back to Chapter F: 'Feedback', remember how important it is to give feedback to people, and use the strategies in Chapter P: 'Poor performance' on how to improve the less acceptable areas of their work.

---

There are many ways for managers to give rewards and recognition to well-performing team members. These should accurately reflect the effort and achievements of the employee, or they can be demotivating.

---

# X: eXtra effort

*All one has to do is hit the right keys at the right time and
the instrument plays itself.*

Johann Sebastian Bach

---

Alan and his team of ten people had been warned
to expect mass redundancies. On crunch day,
one by one, the phones of Alan's team rang and
team members made their way, heads down, to
a meeting room, knowing they would be unlikely
ever to return to their desks. By the end of the day, having
felt physically sick every time their phones had rung, just
Alan and three other members of the team remained.

As Alan arrived the next day at work, he walked into an
eerily empty office and the realization hit him that there was
still the same amount of work to do, but now there were
only four people left.

Senior management had also realized this, so had to
come up with a strategy to motivate people to 'pull out
all the stops' and keep up business as usual. They had
organized a compulsory morale-building event after work
the following week. As times were economically tough,
employees would each be required to pay £40 to cover the
cost of the event.

It was Alan's wife's birthday that night, so the icing on the cake after a horrendous month was that he was forced to miss his wife's birthday and pay for the privilege of it. The atmosphere at the function was anything but high morale.

Alan left the organization a month later. While fearing redundancy he had applied for another job and was eventually offered it. Far from motivating him to work harder, senior management had merely convinced him that getting out was the best option. The very people that management had selected and entrusted to work hard in order to ensure the organization's survival were walking out of the door.

---

 What management initiatives have you experienced or heard of that were designed to motivate people to work harder but had no impact – or the opposite effect?

---

In a difficult economic climate, managers need their employees to try their very hardest, going above and beyond the call of normal duty (sometimes in the face of lower financial reward) and to remain committed to their organization through tough times. So what strategies can managers use that actually work? The answer lies in an approach called **employee engagement**.

## What is employee engagement?

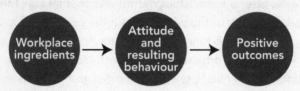

Employee engagement is best described as a set of *workplace ingredients* (also known as 'levers') that positively influence the *attitude* of the employee, which leads to a display of desirable *behaviour*, which leads to *positive outcomes* for the organization.

We will look at these elements in turn, working backwards along the chain.

## Positive outcomes

Compared to disengaged employees, engaged employees:

- Try 57% harder*
- Are 87% less likely to want to leave your organization*
- Are 18% more productive**
- Are 12% more profitable**
- Have 62% fewer accidents**
- Steal 51% less company inventory**
- Take 57% fewer sick days.***

---

\* Corporate Leadership Council, 'Driving employee performance and retention through engagement' (2004).
\*\* Gallup Organization (2006), 'Engagement predicts earnings per share'.
\*\*\* *Engaging for Success* (2008), a report to the government by David MacLeod and Nita Clarke

You can see why many managers are hungry to reap the benefits of having engaged employees. So let's now explore the attitude and resulting behaviour that leads to these positive outcomes.

## Attitude and resulting behaviour

Let's compare the attitude and behaviours of three types of employees: engaged, not engaged and disengaged.

### 1. Engaged employees

| Attitude | Behaviour |
|---|---|
| • Value and enjoy their work.<br>• Feel emotionally attached to the team and organization.<br>• Believe that they will benefit by putting a lot of effort in. | • Willingly work extra hours.<br>• Make every effort to do the best possible job.<br>• Will go beyond what is expected when required. |

Remember Louisa from Chapter W: 'Well done', who did twice as many training courses as her peers? Initially she was a highly engaged employee. Louisa loved her work and believed that her efforts were beneficial to her customers. She did masses of overtime, staying away overnight and working really long days to get great results for her customers, and took pride that this reflected very positively on her team.

## 2. Not engaged employees

| Attitude | Behaviour |
|---|---|
| • Experience less satisfaction from doing day-to-day work.<br>• Feel lower levels of commitment to their team and organization.<br>• Happy to 'coast'. | • Do the minimum needed to produce acceptable work.<br>• Are unwilling to put themselves out for the benefit of the team.<br>• Sit back and let others go above and beyond the call of duty. |

Over time, Louisa stopped feeling engaged. She felt 'burnt out' with her work and made a deliberate decision to try less hard, doing the minimum acceptable level of work. Where she once would have volunteered to help out, she decided to let her peers pick up the additional work for a change.

## 3. Disengaged employees

| • Attitude | • Behaviour |
|---|---|
| • Deeply unhappy at work.<br>• Can have feelings of wanting the team or organization to fail.<br>• Feel no obligation whatsoever towards the team. | • Constantly Against Virtually Everything (also known as 'CAVE' dwellers).<br>• Infect others with their negativity.<br>• May attempt to sabotage the efforts of others. |

Jane was clearly miserable at work. She spoke only to her friends and ignored everyone else. One day, Jane was overheard ringing a customer and deliberately 'badmouthing' her manager, having said that everything was fine in front of the manager. Whenever her team made a suggestion to her, she always began her reply with, 'My concern is ...' or 'I don't think that will work because ...'. Jane's attitude began to have a really toxic impact on the rest of the team, whose morale was dragged down.

---

Think of times in your own working life or that of people you know, that fit each of these three categories. Which category do you feel that you currently sit in?

---

Hopefully you can see the clear link between the attitude and behaviour of engaged employees and the positive outcomes listed above. For example, you can see why someone who is striving to do the best possible job wouldn't cut corners, would concentrate hard, and would therefore be less likely to have an accident. Conversely, you can see why someone who is deeply unhappy about their work and feels no obligation to their team might take more time off sick.

We've aimed to build a case that if you want to reap the positive outcomes of employee engagement you need to influence the attitude of the employees. So, the million-dollar question is: How exactly do you do that?

## Workplace ingredients that lead to engaged employees

Wouldn't it be fantastic if there was just one 'lever' that managers could pull, and all of a sudden employees would be engaged and trying 57% harder than before?

Unfortunately, there isn't one single thing that makes employees feel engaged. The 2004 Corporate Leadership Council's study (referenced above) defined over 300 different levers, categorized into eight key areas:

1. Qualities of the direct manager
2. Qualities of the senior executive team
3. Compensation plans
4. Benefit plans
5. Onboarding (induction)
6. Day-to-day work
7. Learning and development
8. Organizational culture.

So the factors that can influence employee engagement extend well beyond the reach of the direct line manager. However, what was fascinating about the study was that from the top 50 levers that had the biggest impact on employee engagement (and therefore prompted employees to put in extra effort), 36 came from the direct line manager category. So it's clear that managers have a big impact on how people feel at work and the results they generate. You may well be able to identify with this in your own career. For so many people that we have spoken to, it's their manager who makes or breaks their job.

## How can managers increase employee engagement?

The good news is that most of the topics discussed in this book are levers of employee engagement that managers can influence. We've included a table below of examples of some of the levers, shown with the chapter headings.

| Chapter | Example lever |
|---|---|
| Basics | Ensuring employees understand what is expected of them and what they are responsible for doing. |
| Communication | Ensuring that all relevant information is shared and that information is passed both upwards to management and downwards to the employee. |
| Distributing work | Assigning tasks, identifying necessary deadlines and ensuring that employees know how to complete their task. |
| Empowerment | Putting trust in the employees that they will do their job and giving them a sense of control and autonomy over their tasks. |
| Feedback | Giving relevant and informative feedback, both formal and informal. |
| Goal-setting | Agreeing performance expectations to evaluate the effectiveness of the employee. |

| Hiring | Making sure that the right candidates are recruited into the right roles. |
|---|---|
| Induction | Familiarizing the employee with the organization, colleagues, resources and work as early as possible. |
| Justice | Treating team members in a fair manner. |
| Kindness | Demonstrating consideration for employees. |
| Life–work balance | Valuing the balance between work and life of employees. |
| Managing change | Management is sensitive when the organization is required to change. |
| Not coping | Ensures employees are capable of completing the tasks assigned to them and that they have sufficient rest to minimize stress levels. |
| Operational problems | Assisting employees to apply the right solutions to their problems. |
| Poor performance | Holding employees accountable for their performance. |
| Quarrels | Appropriately handling arguments and crisis situations. |
| Respect | Showing that managers are honest and act with integrity. |
| Strengths | Allowing the employee to do what they do best. |
| Training | Giving employees the opportunity to learn from a mentor, receiving sufficient training. |

| Upward progression | Committing to employee personal development plans and accurately evaluating employee potential for growth. |
| Values | Showing respect for employees as individuals and recognizing what they value most. |
| Well done | Appropriately recognizing and rewarding employee achievements. |

What's even better is that most of the levers don't actually cost anything – it doesn't cost managers money to ensure that employees understand what is expected from them, yet managers can reap financial benefits in terms of increased productivity from ensuring that these criteria are met.

**TRY IT NOW!** Run down the levers in the table above and evaluate whether your own manager is satisfying each lever.

Then, if you are currently managing people, evaluate how well you think that you are pulling the levers that will influence people to be engaged.

**IF YOU REMEMBER ONE THING** Employees may well be able to do their jobs, but the commitment that they put into the organization depends on their level of engagement – as their manager, you are in charge of many of the levers that influence this.

# Y: Your personality

*The meeting of two personalities is like the contact of two chemical substances; if there is any reaction, both are transformed.*

Carl Jung

Whereas Chapter V: 'Values' looked at the importance of a person's values at work, this chapter looks in detail at another layer of our onion – your personality.

Even before we arrive at work, our personality is making an impact. Some of us will naturally be running late, others of us are always early. Some people get aggravated in traffic, others sing along happily with the radio. As we walk into our place of work, some stop and chat, others prefer to 'put their heads down' and start working. Some of us like changing desks and sitting with new people, others hate it.

As we interact with each other all day, a unique cocktail of personality preferences is kicking in. Some areas are in harmony, others grate. Everyone is different, and it's natural to work better with some people than others.

You carry your personality around with you *all of the time*, from the moment you wake up in the morning until the moment you fall asleep at night. It has a massive impact upon how we complete our work tasks and what people think of us, yet very often we don't even think about it. When you see your colleagues in the morning, you don't typically think, 'Oh I'm an extravert, therefore I must chat to my colleagues this morning.' You simply are the way that you are.

So, who *are* you? Let's have a go at finding out!

---

TRY IT NOW!
Complete this short personality assessment about you.

There are nine personality scales in the assessment. Each scale has two extreme descriptions of how you could behave (numbered 1 and 5). If you feel that you fit one of these descriptions well, give yourself a 1 or 5 as appropriate. If you are a mixture of the two descriptions, give yourself a rating between 2 and 4 as appropriate. (Please note that 1 does not mean 'bad' and 5 'good' or vice versa. Simply decide a rating that best describes you.)

| Description of a 1 | | Description of a 5 |
|---|---|---|
| I work best independently, being given a task then having the freedom to work on it in my own way and making my own decisions. | | I am a great team player, preferring to produce work collaboratively and discuss ideas and decisions with peers. |
| I work best when I can get started on a project early, so I thrive when I can make slow and steady progress towards a deadline, avoid-ing last-minute pressure. | | I work best with last-minute pressure, so thrive when left to manage my own time and work hard to meet the deadline as it's approaching. |

| | | |
|---|---|---|
| I enjoy detailed planning. | | I find detailed planning over-the-top. |
| I would describe myself as a very quiet individual at work. | | I would describe myself as a very outgoing individual at work. |
| In meetings I prefer to listen to other people's points of view and to accommodate others' points of view rather than voicing my own. | | In meetings I am vocal and very forceful with my points of view and prefer to voice rather than listen to opinions. |
| I like to be constantly stretched and challenged and really enjoy working outside of my comfort zone. | | I am happiest when working well within my comfort zone, completing familiar tasks to a high standard. |
| I would be described as serious at work, focusing hard on the task at hand. | | I would be described as a 'fun' member of the team, who balances getting the job done with creating an enjoyable atmosphere. |
| I prefer to have my personal achievements privately rewarded. | | I prefer to have my personal achievements publicly rewarded. |
| I work best when I am left to put the pressure on myself to get things done and try my hardest. | | I work best when someone else puts the pressure on me to keep going and try my hardest. |

## Great managers know their team members' preferences and adapt to them

So, knowing your own preferences is the first step. The second step is to know the preferences of the people you are managing. People can have very different combinations of scores on this test. Where they are similar to yours – for example, if you both prefer a serious working environment – then you may work more compatibly. However, if you like things to be serious, when your team members thrive on a balance of fun and work, things may not run so smoothly.

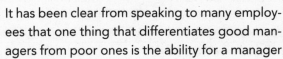 It has been clear from speaking to many employees that one thing that differentiates good managers from poor ones is the ability for a manager to be flexible in their style. This is where a manager moves away from their own personality preferences in order to meet the preferences of different people in their team.

For example, Marie said that she has two very different characters in her team. 'One person wants me to tell them what to do and then to let them go away and do it. Another wants much more hand-holding and constant reassurance that they are on track.' Marie's own preference would naturally be to let them go away and have a go. But she recognizes that in order to bring out the best in the team member who wants more support, she needs to depart from her natural management style. Also, she made a great point that if she suddenly switched around her management style between the two individuals, it would be a disaster. The first person would feel micro-managed and the second person would feel abandoned and would be anxious about how they were progressing.

---

- Ask your team members to complete the above questionnaire (or if you don't have any, you could try this for fun on a partner or someone you work closely with). Alternatively, work out where you think they sit on the scales.
- Look for areas of similarity and areas of difference with your own scores.
- Think about how the similarities and differences have led to positive or negative interactions.

---

## Appreciate the impact (good and bad) that your personality has on others

As well as knowing your own preferences and adapting your management style to bring out the best in your team by meeting their preferences, as a manager you also need to understand the impact that your attitude and behaviour have on other people.

Caroline talked about the difference in her own performance under different managers. One manager had a temperament that was 'highly strung'. Given that Caroline herself has a tendency to worry, her manager's personality exacerbated her own anxiety and she often felt stressed during working hours. She then was managed by a second individual who was much calmer – in Caroline's own words, 'he was serious about what he was doing, but laid back at the same time, and he let me put the pressure on myself. His attitude made me calm.'

If you see your team members behaving in a way that isn't ideal, then it's always worth asking yourself: 'Is there something I can do to change the way I behave and manage my employees to bring out the best in them?' It's certainly much easier to adapt your own behaviour than to try to force someone else to change, and if you don't like the results you're getting, the best place to look for change is **you**.

## Can I change the way that I am?

Pick up a pen and sign your name. How does it feel? Next, put the pen into the other hand and sign your name again. How does it feel?

In that exercise you probably noticed how strange it feels to sign your name with the opposite hand to normal. You probably had to really concentrate on what you were doing. Perhaps the results weren't so great, but over time, if you practised, you'd probably get quite good.

This is an analogy for personality. For example, if you're someone who naturally walks into the office and avoids chit-chat, it would feel strange to try to make small talk. But, crucially, you would be able to do it. Our behaviour isn't set in stone. We might feel a little awkward changing from our normal ways, and we have to make a conscious effort, but we *can* do it.

So the first step to changing our behaviour is to become conscious of how we behave and the impact that our personality is having on others. For example, if you're normally quite dominant in a team meeting and are vocal with your views and you can see people looking frustrated, consciously try to adapt your behaviour to be less forceful – and see how that influences the results you get.

---

 There's one thing that affects everything you do at work, and that is *your* personality. Make sure you use it to bring out the best in those around you.

---

# Z: Zone of successful management

*Teamwork is the ability to work together toward a common vision. The ability to direct individual accomplishments toward organizational objectives. It is the fuel that allows common people to attain uncommon results.*

Andrew Carnegie

This inspirational quote reflects three key elements of management:

1. Achieving the required work output (**task**) through
2. Creating a group that works collectively (**team**) and
3. Directing and nurturing individual efforts (**individual**).

Management guru John Adair depicts these key areas in a useful diagram of three overlapping circles. He concludes that effective managers are not only in control of each of the three individual elements, but crucially they are able to create the right *balance* between them.

---

Being a good manager requires you to operate in the **middle zone** of the three overlapping circles.

---

So let's explore the contents of the three circles in more detail.

1.  **The task**
- Ensuring that working conditions allow the task to be completed.
- Securing the resources needed to complete the work.
- Creating a plan to complete the required work.
- Defining and ensuring acceptable standards of work.
- Reviewing the output of work against the planned schedule and making adjustments where necessary.

2.  **The team**
- Developing a spirit of cooperation whereby team members work to achieve shared goals.
- Removing barriers or resolving conflicts that hinder the team in its collective work.
- Creating a respectful working environment.
- Creating a group of people with appropriate skill-sets, who contribute fairly to complete the team's work.

3.  **The individual**
- Agreeing and reviewing individual responsibilities and output.
- Recognizing and praising individual achievements.
- Assisting with personal and work-related issues.
- Where appropriate, providing extra responsibility and opportunities for progression.
- Understanding team members as individuals: their personality, strengths, goals and values.

Although it may be a little daunting to accomplish all of these management activities, the aim of this Practical Guide has been to break down the complex web of activities into a checklist of simple, bite-sized chunks. Here's a summary of our A–Z to management that supports you in your quest to be a great manager and helps you get into the zone of successful management.

A. Regular self-**assessment** and collection of survey data from your team is a great way to celebrate your strengths, highlight weaker areas so that you can act on them, and keep in touch with how your team are feeling.

B. Make sure that the **basics** are in place. The team must know what is expected of them and have adequate resources and working conditions to complete their tasks.

C. **Communication** affects virtually everything that we do at work and can have a big impact on how we make other people feel. So make sure that your communications are helping, not hindering, your staff.

D. When **distributing work** make sure that it's divided fairly among your team members and that your work-flow management keeps your customers satisfied.

E. **Empowerment** can bring workplace satisfaction for both staff and management, but managers should empower on a case-by-case basis, depending on the person's level of skill and will.

F. Timely **feedback** is vital to keep your team motivated and performing tasks to high standards.

G. Set **goals**, or objectives, that align organizational/team success with individual success, and agree the specifics on how this can be achieved.

H. Follow the seven steps to **hiring**. Have a business case; create a job description; create a person specification; source candidates; draw up a shortlist; assess applicants; make a decision and communicate it.

I. **Inductions** can add a lot of value if done right. Strive to give the new employee a good first impression of the organization by following our induction checklist.

J. Treat people **justly**. Ensure that the amount of work they put in roughly equals the reward that they get back, and that their ratio of input to output is broadly similar to other people doing similar work.

K. Employees will bring their problems into the office. Where a manager shows **kindness** to the member of staff experiencing a personal problem, they will develop trust and a stronger relationship with that individual.

L. Monitor and support the **life–work balance** of your staff. If it tips too much and for too long into a work–work relationship the employee, and ultimately the organization, will suffer.

M. When **managing change** remember to help people to see the positives of change, get them involved in solving problems, support individuals through the change curve, make fair decisions and give your team timely information.

N. Everybody has a limit to the amount of stress that they can endure. Managers should monitor work-related stress levels and take action to support individuals who are **not coping**.

O. When facing **operational problems**, managers must be clear about their boundaries of responsibility, knowing whether it's appropriate for them to take action to resolve them or whether they need to escalate the issue.

P. Where a member of staff is **poorly performing**, ensure that they know this and offer them ways to improve, focusing on their will and skill levels.

Q. **Quarrels** and conflicts can be overcome by applying conflict-handling styles, understanding what it is you want and what the other person wants.

R. Managers have a responsibility to all staff to create a safe workplace founded on **respect**, free from bullying and harassment of any kind.

S. Wherever possible, focus on identifying **strengths** in yourself and among team members and play to them. Individuals, teams and organizations will reap the benefits as a result.

T. Where there is a need or an opportunity for skills, knowledge, attitudes, or behaviour to be developed, a form of **training** can provide a solution, as long as it's well applied.

U. There are various things that you can do to support the **upward progression** of your team members, such as making them a deputy manager, exposing them to senior management activities, finding secondment opportunities or having a mentor.

V. Our **values** underlie our personality and our behaviour. Everybody's will be different, so as a manager it's important you understand what these are and help people find ways to satisfy them.

W. Reward and recognition strategies (saying '**Well done**') have the power to both motivate and demotivate people, so use them carefully. When money is tight, remember the power of non-monetary rewards.

X. Use employee engagement strategies to drive **eXtra effort** from your employees to maximize the performance of your team.

Y.  There's one thing that affects everything you do at work, and that is **your personality**. Make sure you use it to bring out the best in those around you.

Z.  To be a competent manager you have to operate in the **zone** of successfully balancing the needs of the task, the team and the individual. Being able to do this is the mark of a successful manager.

We wish you every success in your current and future management roles and hope that our A–Z of management helps you to get great results on the survey question 'My manager is a good manager'!

# Acknowledgements

Our thanks to Alison's sister and unofficial proofreader, Jacqueline Hardt, for scrutinizing and enjoying the first draft of our book.

Chapter B contains a quote from Garrison Wynn (www.keynote-speaker-motivational.com).

Chapter M – with thanks to the Elizabeth Kubler-Ross Foundation for their permission to describe the Change Curve Theory.

Chapter N contains public sector information (Indicator Tool) published by the Health and Safety Executive and licensed under the Open Government Licence v1.0.

Chapter O – with thanks to Kenneth Thomas and Ralph Kilmann for their permission to describe the five conflict-handling styles.

Chapter S – with thanks to Belbin Associates for permission to describe the Belbin Team Role Theory (www.belbin.com).

Chapter Z – with thanks to John Adair for permission to describe his three-circle model 'Action-Centred Leadership'. More information on this model can be found in one of his books, e.g. Adair, J.E. (1973), *Action-Centred Leadership*, McGraw-Hill, London.